The Crucified Jesus Is No Stranger

REVISED EDITION

Sebastian Moore
FOREWORD BY Joseph Melling

Paulist Press
New York / Mahwah, NJ

The Scripture quotations contained herein are from the New Revised Standard Version: Catholic Edition, Copyright © 1989 and 1993, by the Division of Christian Education of the National Council of the Churches of Christ in the United States of America. Used by permission. All rights reserved.

Quotations from *The Family Reunion* and *Collected Poems 1909–1962* by T. S. Eliot are reprinted by permission from Faber and Faber Ltd. and Harcourt Brace Jovanovich, Inc. The poem "I Am the Great Sun (from a Normandy crucifix of 1632)" by Charles Causley is reprinted with permission from David Higham Associates. Quotations from the play *The Masque of Mercy* by Robert Frost are reprinted by permission from Henry Holt and Company, Inc.

Cover art: "Crucifixion" from The Stations of the Cross painted by Ben Denison (c. early 1960s). Commissioned by St. Isaac Jogues Catholic Church, Niles, Illinois. Used with permission.
Cover and book design by Lynn Else

Library of Congress Cataloging-in-Publication Data
Names: Moore, Sebastian, 1917–2014, author.
Title: The crucified Jesus is no stranger / Sebastian Moore ; foreword by Joseph Melling.
Description: Revised Edition. | New York : Paulist Press, 2018.
Identifiers: LCCN 2018009186 (print) | LCCN 2018032397 (ebook) | ISBN 9781587687914 (ebook) | ISBN 9780809154111 (pbk. : alk. paper)
Subjects: LCSH: Meditations.
Classification: LCC BX2182.3 (ebook) | LCC BX2182.3 .M66 2018 (print) | DDC 242—dc23
LC record available at https://lccn.loc.gov/2018009186

ISBN 978-0-8091-5411-1 (paperback)
ISBN 978-1-58768-791-4 (e-book)

Published by Paulist Press
997 Macarthur Boulevard
Mahwah, New Jersey 07430

www.paulistpress.com

Printed and bound in the
United States of America

I am the great sun, but you do not see me,
  I am your husband, but you turn away.
I am the captive, but you do not free me,
  I am the captain you will not obey.

I am the truth, but you will not believe me,
  I am the city where you will not stay,
I am your wife, your child, but you will leave me,
  I am the God to whom you will not pray.

I am your counsel, but you do not hear me.
  I am the lover whom you will betray.
I am the victor, but you do not cheer me,
  I am the holy dove whom you will slay.

I am your life, but if you will not name me,
Seal up your soul with tears and never blame me.

—From "I Am the Great Sun
(from a Normandy Crucifix of 1632)"
by Charles Causley

CONTENTS

Contents

FOREWORD

Opening the pages of Sebastian Moore's most celebrated book, we are surprised by the freshness of the writing and the zestful spirit of inquiry that illuminates his text. Written almost half a century ago, *The Crucified Jesus Is No Stranger* challenges us to meet with God on personal terms and to understand Jesus as the embodiment of the humanity to whom we might aspire.

The author of this remarkable text illustrates a process of estrangement from God and each other, arising from a defect in understanding our own worth in the eyes of a living and loving God. This betrayal of our destiny was sealed by an abiding fear of death and an escape into an unreal, self-defeating cycle of living, allowing a sinful evasion of God's love in a narcissistic gratification of insecure, selfish needs. The good news brought by Jesus was that this violation of our destiny could be overcome through the love of God and his people. Christ's mission was imperative: the gulf between humanity and God lay not merely in man's alienation from his only salvation, but also because the idea of a perfect being—remote from the travails of worldly struggle—had removed God to an impersonal, untouchable realm, apparently beyond the capacity of human beings to encounter. There was a danger that traditional accounts of Jesus as a perfect being, Godlike in his capacity as Savior, could similarly distance us from the world of Christ as a human being. Moore's primary concern in this book is to reinstate the personhood of Jesus, reiterating that we need to recover the message of Jesus as a person who could translate into the language of his contemporaries the depth of God's love for humanity. For the remainder of his life, this Benedictine monk was absorbed with the personal, human impact of Jesus on the first disciples and upon us as their modern counterparts.

In seeking to convey a sense of personal intimacy with Jesus, Moore offers an interesting but hardly radical contribution to the theology of our world. The novel quality provided by *The Crucified Jesus* lies not in the recognition of Jesus, the man, but rather in the way the author seeks to map out the spiritual journey undertaken by the first Christians, in intellectual and spiritual terms which we can comprehend today. How does he achieve this and what is the quality of the analysis which he offers us? We might answer simply that Moore demonstrates that the resurrection of Jesus had proved to his followers that death can be overcome and the ancient fear of mortality, which was also an expression of humanity's desperate, sinful quest to avoid God's commandments, could be transcended. Such a bland answer would obscure the radical intent of this book as it sought to confront several problems which the Catholic Church faced in the late twentieth century, and which remain today. Moore is doing much more than offering traditional arguments in a fresh language—a younger wineskin. The text speaks to several concerns of the book's initial audience. His analysis offers not an emotive appeal to identify with the intense suffering of a blameless man executed unjustly for reasons of political expediency in the Palestine of the Roman Empire. *The Crucified Jesus* is more interested in the psychic and spiritual impact of Jesus on those around him, conveying the sense of shock which swept over his followers as their charismatic teacher and leader was physically degraded and destroyed by the authorities. To understand Moore's work more fully, we can consider the main intellectual influences evident in his writing and the place of this book in his own journey as a priest and a spiritual teacher.

INSPIRATIONS FOR A JOURNEY

There is little doubt that Moore's writing was strongly colored by the ideas of the Canadian Jesuit, Bernard Lonergan, whose book *Insight* (1957) made a deep impression on Moore—and on his abbot at Downside, Christopher Butler, who was to become a luminary of the Second Vatican Council. One of the attractions of Lonergan's efforts to "modernize" the philosophic foundations of Thomas Aquinas was his confident engagement with a wide range of scientific and human disciplines. Moore clearly preferred a searching investigation of the material world to the idealism of St. Augustine, though in contrast to many of his Downside contemporaries, he had shown surprisingly little interest in earlier efforts by Teilhard de Chardin to reconcile evolutionary theory and Christian thinking.[1]

After his immigration to the United States in 1971, Moore became an active member of the Lonergan workshops in Milwaukee and Boston. Addressing a commemorative gathering in Rome, he deplored the relative neglect into which his master's ideas had fallen by the end of the century.[2] It is curious that the author of *The Crucified Jesus* makes little direct reference to Lonergan, in contrast to theologians such as Rahner and Bultmann, as well as the much-admired Ernest Becker.[3] Moore was later to apply part of Lonergan's methodology to his own psychoanalytic interpretation of literary classics, though he makes little attempt here to link his ideas to the Jungian concepts that informed his work. Moore's decision not to uncover this intellectual groundwork in extensive references to theological authorities helps to explain the cool, sometimes skeptical, reception given to his books in academic circles, even extending to sympathetic readers such as his nephew Nicholas Lash.[4] On reflection, we may say that the discursive style of explanation in the present text brings arguments together by a brilliant fusion of concepts and insights taken from a range of disciplines, making unexpected connections to construct a fresh reading of familiar passages. The resulting hybrid form of analysis sparkles with innovative thinking, even though it may lack the heavy ballast of systematic proofs demanded by professional theologians.

Moore's apparent neglect of the usual infrastructure of theological references did not arise from mere indolence or an impatience with academic apparatus: he frankly admits in his introduction that he offers "only a series of hints, not a system of theology to be taken over." The author invites readers to develop their own insights, based on sure foundations of their experience, just as his own "inertia-shifting insights" arose from personal discoveries.[5]

Moore shared with the American Trappist monk, Thomas Merton, a desire to write books on theological questions, while feeling inadequate to the task of encompassing all the necessary reading. Each was more strongly drawn to the mystical works of St. John of the Cross than "undigestible material."[6] Another shared delight was the writing of poetry and the voracious consumption of imaginative literature, several of his own poems being included in Moore's first major work, *God Is a New Language*. Moore considered poetry to elicit those liminal thoughts and insights that bordered on the edge of the conscious mind, but which offered flashes of light on the other inarticulate expressions of the soul in search of spiritual fulfillment. Among the great religious poetry for which he retained a lifelong passion was the Song of Songs in the Old Testament and the writings of St. John of the Cross, who translated the Song of Songs into Spanish and composed the famous *Dark Night of the Soul*.

If Lonergan was one genius whom he acknowledged as a seminal influence on his thinking, F. R. Leavis, whom he met almost two decades before he traveled to Rome to study with Lonergan in 1959, was another. During the Second World War, Moore, a young Benedictine novice, read English literature at

Cambridge, where Leavis encouraged his passionate interest in T. S. Eliot, the impress of whose spiritual poetry can be seen throughout the present book.[7] In *The Crucified Jesus*, Moore quotes Robert Frost and other authors to illustrate his ideas, though he does not venture deeply into the theoretical tools needed to explore fully the connections between imaginative literature and mystical experience. His later writings on Shakespearean drama integrated his analysis of verse drama in an interpretation which combined Lonergan's ideas with those of Freudian (and Jungian) psychoanalytic theory.[8]

Among the gifts which the poetry of Eliot, among others, gave to Moore was a powerful sense of place in locating the moment of spiritual experience—most famously in *The Four Quartets*. Moore shared again with Merton a deep admiration for Abbot John Chapman, though he struggled to follow the more formal exercises of contemplative "mental" prayer prescribed at Downside.[9] In September 1944, he experienced a profound moment of revelation during one such struggle to pray at the abbey. He called out in exasperation to God and soon fell into a trance of mystical love with God. Famously indifferent to his physical surroundings, Moore vividly recalled this specific experience of loving surrender against a backdrop of golden flowers in the autumn sunshine as he walked in the abbey grounds before vespers. The poetic quality of the mystical moment when the monk engaged directly with God is a testimony to the seminal importance of a revelation which Moore considered the defining point of his life. He was able to combine this sense of personal mystery with an urgent appeal for us to understand our experience of Jesus, and of God, with a freshness that makes the historical experience of the Savior a matter of tangible and immediate interest to us today.

Joseph Melling
April 6, 2018

NOTES

1. Teilhard de Chardin had a major impact on Luke Suart, a close contemporary of Moore's.

2. For reference to Moore's address at the Gregorian University, see *The Realms of Desire: An Introduction to the Thought of Bernard Lonergan* (Washington DC: Woodstock Theological Center, 2011), 4. https://www.lonerganresource.com/pdf/books/4/The%20Realms%20of%20Desire%20-%20An%20Introduction%20to%20the%20Thought%20of%20Bernard%20Lonergan.pdf.

3. Cf. 30–31, 43, 69. The appendix on self-discovery was a Lonergan workshop paper of 1976, 95–116.

4. Nicholas Lash was the first Catholic to hold a chair of theology at Cambridge since the Reformation. Private communication to present author.

5. Cf. xii.

6. Thomas Merton, *The Sign of Jonas* (London: Burns & Oates, 1953), 173 ("Feast of St. Robert, April 29, 1949").

7. Cf. 70, for example.

8. Glenn Hughes and Sebastian Moore, "*Hamlet* and the Affective Roots of Decision: A Dramatic Specification of Bernard Lonergan," *Lonergan Workshop*, vol. 7, edited by Fred Lawrence (Atlanta: Scholars Press, 1988), 179–202.

9. Merton, *The Sign of Jonas*, 236 ("September 13, 1949"), for Chapman's *Spiritual Letters*. Moore edited a later edition of the *Letters*.

INTRODUCTION

For many years, I have had a special concern with Christology. I have always had a pressing sense of the *contrast* between Jesus and culture. I felt that this contrast was always being blurred by theologians, by piety, by all the Christian worlds of discourse. It seemed that we were all having it both ways: worshipping a Jesus who at once turns the world upside down and takes his place within it, still the old way up.

I was especially drawn to those few courageous men and women whose commitment to Jesus set them at odds with society and its norms and expectations. It was in such confrontations that a new Christology would be born, a newly marked Christology of contrast.

Contrast. It gave to Jesus many names in my thinking, some named, some only implied: "challenger," "questioner," "outsider," "prophet," "poet," "revolutionary," "protester."

I began to see that the great contrast between Jesus and normality, that I had for so long felt in my bones, gave to him a more mysterious name that I had been *resisting* in my bones: the name of "victim." Everything changed.

I remembered how, long ago, I had wandered with some friends into a country church near Rome. It was the Feast of the Sacred Heart, and they were singing the first anthem of Vespers: "One of the soldiers opened his side with a spear, and immediately there came out blood and water." Quietly, and with a part of the mind that does not wrestle with concepts, I knew that the whole thing was there: the act of aggression, of sin, releasing the waters of grace. This holistic vision, this symbolic concentration of truth, I experienced and was nourished by—and promptly forgot—for nearly fifteen years.

With the realization that Jesus had to be seen above all as victim, the cumbersome work of the intellect caught up with, and became caught up in, that moment in the country church. The intellectual work was not denied but deepened. That affair of man with Jesus, of man-in-society with this new possibility of man, was at its center a confrontation of bitterness, of sorrow, and of healing. It was a healing of the mind when the traditional language—"done to death for our sins"—came at me in a new way: no longer as some sort of transposed application to "the Christ-event" of a primitive idea of expiation, but as the meaning of the contrast between Jesus and culture. In my thinking, the language of Jesus as the saving victim rose from the dead—and so did my Christian mind.

The most important concept to revive in me was the concept of sin, which, like the concept of victim, now came to me in the context of the vision of man that I had been building up over the years. I began to see, at the heart of, and as the explanation of, the whole complex human phenomenon, an unconscious refusal, a failure of man to come to some great meeting place, a stopping short. At its root unconscious, it was a very powerful refusal, a refusal powered by a nameless and pervasive fear. A refusal so powerful, so influential of all behavior, so unreachable in its roots, that even the fear that powers it seldom goes by that name.

"What is it that we are refusing?" was the next question. What we are refusing is not, directly at least, "obedience to God" but some fullness of life to which God is impelling us and which our whole being dreads. Some unbearable personhood, identity, freedom, whose demands beat on our comfortable anonymity and choice of death. Furthermore, something that at root we *are*, a self that is ours yet persistently ignored in favor of the readily satisfiable needs of the ego.

Then there began to emerge an idea that would prove to be the linchpin. What if Jesus were the representative, the symbol, the embodiment, of this dreaded yet desired self of each of us, this destiny of being human, this unbearable identity and freedom (freedom and identity being really the same thing)? The crucifixion of Jesus then becomes the central drama of a person's refusal of his or her true self. Furthermore, this drama can be seen in two successive situations. First, in its historical incidence, in which it expresses only the *conflict* between normal humanity as handled by the Caiaphases and the Pontius Pilates, and the true being of humanity. Second, and much more importantly, in the experience of the believer, who, confronted with Jesus crucified, finds all the evil in his life becoming *explicit* as the willful destruction of his true self now concrete for him in the man on the cross. Evil made totally explicit is resolved in the forgiveness of God of which the crucifixion thus becomes the symbol and sacrament. All symbols transform. *This* symbol transforms evil into sin and sin into sorrow and forgiveness. Through this conversion, the believer finds as her own that identity that first she rejected and crucified. She passes—and we are forever passing, back and forth—from "crucifying the Lord of glory" to being "nailed to the cross with Christ."

The crucified as a symbol that transforms evil into sin and sin into grace: here surely is the intellectual structure of that vision of the soldier's spear opening the side and releasing the torrent of new life.

This structure illuminates Paul's grand idea in Romans, of sin as *explicit* refusal of God in the *myth* of Adam, as operating *clandestinely* and all-pervasively in *history* (the "culture" of which Jesus must be victim), as imperfectly explicit through the Law, and finally as totally explicit, and so resolved in the love of God, in the crucifixion. I was understanding for the first time the statement, "For our sake he made him to be sin who knew no sin, so that in him we might become the righteousness of God" (2 Cor 5:21).

Next, Ernest Becker's book *The Denial of Death* uncovered for me the roots of that human evil of which the cross is both the dramatization and resolution. That those roots lie deep was well known to Paul. He knew that the evil with which the cross has principally to do lies far beyond what we normally experience as sin, beyond the area that we think of as free choice. Becker showed me that the root is in the very constitution of the human as that evolutionarily bizarre phenomenon, the conscious animal: the animal who, *knowing* his total contingency, turns from it in fear and builds the idolatrous image of himself. The root of all human evil, Becker says, is our necessary attempt to deny our creaturehood. Here was the validation, amazingly simple yet at great depth, of that sense of the human as less than human, of that subhumanity of culture, that had fascinated me for a decade and that was basic to my understanding of Jesus. Here was anthropological justification for the Christian insight that the evil with which God deals in Christ is necessary, a necessary stage in a process of which God is the meaning. Here, in the poignant picture of the conscious and so fearful animal, was the *anthropology* of my idea of God giving humanity a destiny that we could not take and we only come into in a glorious mystery of blood, sorrow, forgiveness, and rebirth.

I considered, then, the crucifixion's resolution of our evil in terms of the symbolism that our evil confers upon death. Our egoistic self-importance leads us to see death, which is simply part of the life process, as the end of what we consider as alone significant, the works of the ego. The death of Jesus, the man without sin, shatters this tragic symbolism and reveals a deeper meaning in death: "return to the Father."

Thus, the primary exercise in which the converted conscious-ness firms itself up is the celebration of the death of the Lord as return to the Father. We affirm our Christian freedom by a rite that flouts our sinful tragic cultural vision of death.

Finally, living with this new vision of the crucified, as I prayed it and shared it, I came to see that it contains a whole ascetico-mystical program. The art of contemplating Jesus cru-cified is to come to understand, in painful situations, that the cross that I always first experience as "life's crucifixion of me" is in reality my crucifixion of life, in other words, the Jesus-cross. There is only one true cross, to which all our "crosses" must be conformed, and this involves not just asking him to help me carry mine, but also *inverting* mine—inverting the roles of crucifier and crucified—to conform to his. The ques-tion "Who is crucifying whom? What is crucifying what?"— asked prayerfully and reflectively—is a talisman for liberating my friends from my tyranny and liberating myself from this tyranny.

Now, in a way, you have read this book! But the main ideas are for the individual to grasp imaginatively, and this the reader will be more able to do by following me in the process of their unearthing.

Moreover, this book is based on my own experience. How much I have allowed my ego to try to persuade you of its truth by making it more tidy and watertight than direct experience ever is or needs to be, I do not know. Therefore, I stress that it is only a series of hints, not a system of theology to be taken over lock, stock, and barrel. I am sure that you will come up with your own, and therefore other, psychic processes in this field, and these are what the book is designed to elicit. In the spiri-tual life, the only motivational and inertia-shifting insights, the only ones that touch us in our indolence and so make a per-manent difference to our lives, are those that have come from ourselves alone, discoveries. Bon voyage, therefore!

One last point. This book would not have been possible without some "revelations" that occurred between myself and some others with whom I worked through the Spiritual Exercises of Ignatius in the role of director. I am eternally grateful to them for what they have shown me of God's ways with men and women in the mystery of Jesus Christ.

Part One

THE CRUCIFIED

1

THE WORST AND THE BEST

No person can say where evil originated in him or her; that is of the essence of evil. Because the *origin* of evil is lost to us, correspondingly obscure to us is the significance of death. Evil is confused, for us, alike in its beginning and in its end.

The crucifixion of Jesus raises this elusive reality called evil to consciousness. In place of the death in which evil *issues*, there is a death that it *causes*. The person who contemplates this event with the vision of faith brings to consciousness the origin of evil within. By an extraordinary paradox, the person's first real conviction that God loves him or her takes place in the context of a self-discovery as a crucifier.

The crucifixion of Jesus dramatizes that in us which is of its nature faceless. Evil is of its nature diffused. It is in the whole human situation. It is in the crucifiers and in the crucified. In *this* crucifixion, however, there are significant changes, (a) *All* humans, the weak as well as the strong, show up as crucifiers, (b) there is *not* evil in the crucified, (c) thus *all* the evil is in the crucifiers, and (d), most difficult to grasp, the evil thus restricted to the crucifiers becomes an *act*, arising in the human heart and proceeding to its destructive conclusion: an *act*, don't you see, and no longer an *atmosphere*. The evil that we experience as a *climate* to which we contribute, becomes, in this august confrontation with the Sinless One crucified, a personal act, a source. The spring of evil becomes conscious and personal in the face of the Crucified, as we know our worst, and know, for the first time, a total acceptance.

The crucifixion of Jesus makes to be *at our hands* that death that is rather our *climate*. That which we kill, in ourselves and in each other, in vicarious and clandestine ways, we have killed once clearly and in the light of day. Death, which is normally a *symbol* of evil, becomes, in this extraordinary instance, evil's *visible effect*. And *this* is the manifestation of God's love: that extraordinary love that highlights our evil to leave us in no doubt that it is accepted.

It is because, in accord with the deepest logic of the psyche, *love* is experienced in the vision of the Crucified. It is because this law of direct ratio between the extent of evil's acting out and the credibility of the accepting love has been obeyed to the uttermost limits, that the psyche has experienced the plunging of the spear into Christ's side *as* the opening up of the well-spring of new life.

2

INCARNATION

Christ is our way to God. We go to the Father through him. These propositions have been translated into a rule for meditation: the believer should learn first to fix one's eye on Christ, so as to be led, in God's time, to the Father.

Experience, my own and others', has taught me that there is another way. This consists in first becoming convinced of God's love as an all-penetrating force. Then coming to experience evil in myself as a reality so pervasive and elusive as to its origin, that I cannot experience *it* as accepted by God in love without the presence of some other factor, in which God's love would *go to meet* my evil. This other factor is the crucifixion and death of Jesus, when this is regarded precisely as "authorized" by God to declare his love for us. For in this conception, God obeys the deepest psychological law of acceptance: to be convinced of my acceptance, I must know that I am accepted at my worst. God shows me to myself as worse than I had ever conceived—a crucifier of the Sinless One—to leave in me no possible room for doubt—no possible *further* experience of evil that might create doubt—that he loves and accepts me.

This imputation of a motive to God for his choice of the cross as a revelatory medium is something of an impertinence. It is perhaps the most rational way of pointing to something that is not rational, namely, why God chose the crucifixion of Jesus in its indivisible totality of crucifiers and crucified, and did not merely "draw good" out of the "antecedently" not-intended evil that brought the Sinless One to the cross. But this idea is only a pointer. In reality, the crucifixion of Jesus stands for a meeting between God and evil that is far beyond our rational grasp and is made known to mystics in those moments of irresponsible love that subvert all normal values.

This way of experiencing Christ as the manifestation of God does not go from Christ to God, but from God to Christ. More precisely, from "God" to "God in the final absurd fact of us," from God generically to God in the ultimate human specific. Here Christ appears not to the gaze of our innocence; his image clears only as our roots in evil are laid bare, when the cost and shape of really believing in a divine lover of men begin to reveal themselves. There follow three considerations.

First, from this new standpoint, the deficiency of the more usual way reveals itself. Standard meditation techniques insist that this man I am contemplating died for me. But this shattering truth is revealed only with the appearance of Christ as God's sign of his acceptance of evil. It is seriously distorted when, transplanted from this dark and fertile spiritual soil, it is made to declare itself in the daylight world of our normal relations. There's John who got you that good job—and there's Jesus who died for you.

Second, if ever there was a man who went this way, that man was Paul. Paul never knew Jesus. But he knew the spiritual man's wrestle with sin, and he resisted, with everything within him, the notion of a God who would undercut this struggle by an all-embracing love. He heard the words "it is hard for you to kick against the goal."

Paul's extreme statements in Romans reflect this vision in which sin dictates the shape of God's love on earth. "For our sake he made him to be sin who knew no sin, so that in him we might become the righteousness of God" (2 Cor 5:21). Only with our sin could God touch us sinners. Only in its form, so inalienably ours, could he appear as our familiar. God made "him to be sin." We have been content to describe this phrase as metaphorical, as an extreme way of putting a truth that lies beyond it. In fact, this statement is not a metaphor but a direct transcript of the *divine use of sin*, and as such is a figure that *contains* the truth. But this truth is essentially something experienced thus "God—sin—Christ—love!" The logic of deep human self-awareness is a logic all its own. It is the creation of a new *space*, with the attendant rule that everything that is to become definitive for us does so by occupying that space. The space is marked "sin." So *there*, and *that*, God's representative must be. Christ is there. Christ is that. This way of thinking is only barbarous for the reason.

Finally, in this way, the mystery of the incarnation is not the imaginable descent of the God into the womb of the Virgin, but rather comes upon us as a being of God in us. The difficulty of the incarnation is not in the dogmatic realm. It is the difficulty in a commanded self-acceptance that goes far beyond our limits of self-acceptance. It is the mystery of a God who comes upon us and loves us beyond the limits of our ego-organized potential.

Christ is our way to the Father only because he is the Father's way to us, the Father's way with us, the mysterious expiation of our sin.

When we say, with the Christmas preface, "that through knowing God visibly we may be brought to the love of things invisible," we must ask, what is made visible in Christ? What is made visible is God's touch in the innermost region of the soul where sin qualifies the old man. And this is the divinity of Christ: for only God can touch us there. He touches us by inundating us in a mystery of incarnation, passion, death, and resurrection.

Humans are incurable optimists. We are impelled to improve on our situation, to "think positively." In this positive thinking, we come upon a God who loves us and who will be our ally in the struggle with our inner chaos. Yet the God who loves us is and will remain the projection of our optimism until he is somehow brought by God to turn about and face the chaos and—far more than this—to recognize that the chaos has a name, a form of its own, a force: the name is sin, the evil of man that resists the love of God. When we praise this love, sin does not contradict us but simply goes underground and continues to belie in hidden ways our belief in God's love. Therefore, the revelatory mystery features, irreducibly, the *two* pairings: *God the Father* and *love*; *Christ* and *sin.* That love is true and not the projection of optimism, only because its obverse is a mystery of blood and expiation. The meeting between these two polarities, of Father-love and Christ-expiation, is the Holy Spirit.

At the deepest point of our adventure with God, we are brought to our own dark mystery, where God's love gets lost in our own tortuous selfhood, when God's love and our own flourishing refuse to coincide, and for a reason that we do not fully understand. At this point, however, God enables us to catch a glimpse of our true self, in which they do coincide, but this true self is separated from us in its beauty, and we find we are its crucifier. With that world that resists the glory, we are allied, as a crucifier. Here is the mystery of blood, and of God's love enfleshed as forgiveness.

If we proceed in this order, starting, that is, with our psychic being, the point at which the Christ-Self begins to be history is just here—where the mystery of blood reveals itself. For the blood, says the psyche, is shed or it is nothing. It is now that the Christ becomes Jesus: on the cross. From the cross, we, as it were, create history backward—down the life of Jesus back to his Virgin birth.

Only the self, God's self, the self-for-God, is crucified, and only by the ego. The pattern is constant. The only variation is that I move from an extroverted position, regarding it, whereby *I* am the crucifier, *he* the crucified, to a centered position where I acquire sufficient *selfhood* to be *identified* with the crucified. This is the transition from one who "crucifies the Lord of Glory" to one who is "nailed to the cross with Christ." It is the same person, changing only through self-discovery in Christ.

3

MAKING PEACE BY THE BLOOD OF HIS CROSS

A further step needs to be taken. I have said that God uses the crucifixion of Jesus to convince us that, even at our worst, as crucifiers of the good, we are accepted by him. Yet this obscures the fact that there is a transcendental relationship between sin in its ultimate manifestation and the love of God. From the more familiar point of view that we have been unfolding, God's forgiveness is greeted, as it occurs in the context of the crucifixion, with the cry "even there!" But from a more radical viewpoint, however, we have to say, "Especially there, essentially there, most clearly there, with finality there, finally there." For evil brought to its essential self-expression necessarily encounters and succumbs to the love of God. Evil, which has always worked its way incognito into the whole life of the individual and society, once it gets inscribed, as it were, on the universe, encounters and is embraced within the love that is all-encompassing. "Ah see, where Christ's blood streams in the firmament!" cries Marlow's *Doctor Faustus*. *That* is the sign of God's all-accepting love, *because* it is the at last adequate sign of evil. The blood that cries to heaven as the true emblem and symbol and meaning of sin calls down the infinite love. Let us consider some alternative wordings for this awesome idea.

In the ultimate order the ultimate sin, of crucifying the Just One, reverses itself, the victim giving life to the crucifiers. Sin, our deep, necessary, negative power, has no being. The only kind of "being" it can have is the sight of itself in its ultimate effect, the crucified. This solution is uniquely God's. It is dimly glimpsed in an ultimate maturity of the spirit. For we must experience God coming into us, taking our shape of sin, making explicit our sin, making sin work our salvation. The ultimate truth, which is God's unique embrace, is that the essential *effect* of sin—the crucified—is, identically, the healing. What sin ultimately *is*, is seen in the crucified. What sin ultimately *is*, is forgiven. For sin brought to its ultimate succumbs to God's love. It cannot be otherwise. It suffices for God to make our elusive evil explicit in crucifixion, for it to be no more. The crucified, therefore, *as* signifying sin's *ultimate* meaning, signifies its *forgiveness*. To *see* sin is to see its forgiveness. Humanity without the Christ cannot see sin, and so cannot see forgiveness.

This radical statement illuminates two great Pauline themes: that of the pervasive and elusive nature of sin until the final démarche when, in the crucifixion of Jesus, it at last finds expression and thus encounters the love of God, and that of the correspondence between Adam and Christ as consisting in the fact that in these two human situations alone sin is out in the open. The two themes combine. We have a picture of man, in his beginning, "having it all together," knowing no split in himself between his creaturehood and his self-actualization (Ernest Becker), or between spontaneity and will (Rahner on "concupiscence"), or between nature and civilization (George B. Leonard and S. Moore), man in such a position, that is, that the admission of evil will have the clear form of rebellion against God. The first sin committed in this condition is the last that will have this clarity until the New Man makes possible the resumption of this ultimate dialogue of man with his God. To describe the nature of sin during this interim is to describe a complex history of disguises, partial disclosures, and correspondingly partial remedies.

This history is one of the themes of Romans. Rahner sums it up thus:

> The Sin which appears in the world and affects all men in consequence of Adam's act is not regarded by St. Paul as a purely static deprivation of the spirit suffered by Adamite man; rather this primal and hereditary sin contains a dynamic and active element which urgently seeks to reveal its own nature in the personal sins of the individual. Thus *the* Sin comes into the world like a ruler (Rom 5:12), "dwells" in man's flesh (Rom 7:20), subjects man to itself as its slave (Rom 6:6,17,20; 7:14), revives through the experience of the Law (Rom 7:8,9), in this way becomes manifest in man's concrete life (Rom 7:13) by subjecting man to its law (Rom 7:23; 8:2) and using his "members" as its weapons (Rom 6:13). (*Theological Investigations*, vol. 1, 347n2)

Situating history as interim between the two clear "men," and the consequent theological symmetry between the two "men," is clearly stated by Paul. The period that best exemplifies the *confusion* that follows the original loss is the period from Adam to Moses. "Yet death exercised dominion from Adam to Moses, even *over those whose sins were not like the transgression of Adam, who is a type of the one who was to come*" (Rom 5:14 [au. emphasis]).

During the period of the Law, evil could once again assume its proper form of "disobeying a direct command," but *this* disobedience was a mere shadow of the clear Adamic disobedience. For this is a situation in which a person, faced with the alternatives of obedience and disobedience, does not know oneself and answers to the classic description in Romans: "For we know that the law is spiritual; but I am of the flesh, sold into slavery under sin. I do not understand my own actions. For I do not do what I want, but I do the very thing I hate. Now if I do what I do not want, I agree that the law is good. But in fact it is no longer I that do it, but sin that dwells within me" (Rom 7:14–17). Sin maintains its diffused and not fully enfleshed condition in us. It has us doing evil, but not through the unambiguous decision of our total being. Just as the disobedience of man under the Law fails to reproduce the disobedience of Adam, so his obedience under the Law fails to be that obedience from which Adam defected. Thus, while what cancels the disobedience of Adam is a new obedience, this is nothing less than the reappearance of the total man amidst the human chaos. In this new context, the obedient man must be crucified by the evil that, incognito, pervades the human. Evil, unmasked as the crucifier of the true man, knows itself for the first time and, for the first time, confronts that which alone prevails over and must prevail over evil, namely, God's love.

Yet the more we succeed in clarifying this Pauline logic, the more we are driven to seek out the *interiority* of the process that it describes. What is it in a person that God seeks, whose flourishing is God's glory, whose neglect seems unavoidable in the self-building of humankind, and whose crucifixion might lay bare what the whole conspiracy of history has hidden, and open the way to a new outpouring of the Spirit of God in human hearts and in human community? What is this center to which Jesus gives expression and calls into existence in a dark mystery of expiation? Who *are* we, that we are *thus* lost, *thus* rediscover ourselves, and are *thus* recovered by an all-encompassing love?

To answer this question is a delicate matter. Yet it is hardly to be doubted that the answer must be on the lines of a distinction between the ego and the self. Generically—and with all the weakness inherent in a generic statement—evil consists in an infinite variety of alienations between the conscious ego of humanity and a total self in which he or she has his or her place in God's world. And so generically, salvation consists in the overcoming of this protean alienation. Yet even apart from the question of its Christological understanding, this generic statement is hedged, for the wise practitioner of Jungian theory, by an almost despairing caution: the person who comes to some sense of what is called the self comes under an almost insuperable temptation to claim this realization "for oneself," to appropriate it in terms of the ego. Such a person becomes the mystagogue for whom the mystery of human totality has become a pretension and has *replaced* the need to live out the life of the ego in its context of history and society. For the wise, on the contrary, the coming into the self is expressed only in silent contemplation, in humility, and in the indefinable benefits that the wise confer on the less aware.

Now this caution, this restricted but most precious application of the paradigm of ego and self, is most eloquently exemplified in our approach to the mystery of Jesus Christ. To come into that mystery, I must give more serious weight than in the Jungian praxis to the fact that I am in large part outside it. The articulation of *this* factor for the Christian, *his or her* way of recognizing the ego in its whole political complex, *his or her* way of not short-circuiting salvation, is to say, I recognize myself, in the total context of this mystery, as the sinner brought to consciousness and sorrow as the crucifier of the self, that is not "my best self" or "my full potential," or any other of our pretentious euphemisms, but is symbolized most truly by a sinless man crucified on a hill, for whose crucifixion I gladly accept liability within a mystery of God's all-encompassing love. As I accept *that* position, in meditation and in the praxis of life, I may be led, in the spiritual logic of the mystery and

14

under the sway of the Spirit, to a growing inward sense of *that which is crucified*. Yet while I live in this world, my life will move—in rhythm with all the complexities of being a participant in the mystery of evil and its redemption—between the poles of crucifier and crucified. In short, the self-experience of the believer as crucifier and crucified is the most acute and committed form of that self-experience between the poles of ego and self that is the fruit of a Jungian self-understanding.

The following lines from Eliot's play *The Family Reunion* provide a poetic summary of the history of sin:

> It is possible that sin may strain and struggle
> In its dark instinctive birth, to come to
>   consciousness
> And *so* find expurgation. (emphasis mine)

4

THE LAMB SLAIN FROM THE FOUNDATION OF THE WORLD

The human has a secret, operative in all that he desires, wills, and creates. It is that, finally, one does not believe in oneself. Balancing all one's achievements, there is the death wish. The latter reaches, in times of crisis and decay like the present, a dangerous degree of overtness. But even in the time of flowering, it was there. Not only do we know that we will die. We let this fact speak to us of the vanity of all that we strive for.

Yet this will-not-to-be is no mere weakness. It *resists* the power that calls us into being and that, in us consciousness, calls us to being, to identity, to personhood, to himself. The will-not-to-be desires to undo the order of being that represents this power, to make it not the case that we are called to an ever-greater intensity of selfhood.

This is the mystery of evil, of which we have many occasions to be conscious. Evil is the inability of the death wish to be simply a death wish: its necessity to justify itself by removing the very *grounds* for requiring of us a more intensely personal life. This shows itself in the resentment that is sometimes felt in the presence of an exceptionally good and courageous person. The desire to remove him or her is the desire to remove an unusually eloquent piece of evidence for the fact that we are called to full personhood. The most passionately protected thing in us is our mediocrity, our fundamental indecision in respect of life. Its protection will require, and will not stop at, murder.

We may think that once this conspiracy of cowardice in the face of being is exposed to us, we would be able to overcome it, but this is not so. This inertial force of evil in us has the power of a fear that we do not understand, a fear that would be overcome only by some extraordinary new birth of love in us, in response to some new revelation.

Christianity offers itself as this revelation, this goal to love. Its way of dissolving the inertia of evil is so simple yet so extraordinary that we are impelled to say that it *is* in the nature of revelation. The resolution consists in provoking us to act out, in a uniquely total way, our desire for the good and the true and the wholly personal not to be there. It presents us with the vision of Jesus, the man without evil in him, destroyed simply because he *is* without evil. It invites us, under the pressure of a new force called Holy Spirit, to discover ourselves in that classic murder and to experience, in this avowed aversion to the good, acceptance of us by the power that makes all things. More essentially, it invites us to experience our evil as never before, at last unmasked, to experience our decent death wish as murder, and *in* that experience to feel for the first time the love that overpowers evil.

Thus, at the threshold of our advance into full personhood, there is not simply a new incentive but a crisis, in which the dark power of evil within us finds at last its appropriate and beautiful object and destroys it. What then? The "what then?" situation does not otherwise arise. When it does, there is and can be only love. Love is that which can only reveal itself to us in the total expenditure of our hatred of being. Only love can be there, and love can only be there.

In this crisis, our identity, which we have shied away from, floods into us on a tide of love. It is only by a total surrender that we come into our identity, a surrender whose dimensions embrace the deep mystery of our refusal and has required, for its being made, the full experience of that refusal. In other words, the beauty into which being-fearful man comes is crucified. The image of the crucified is the glory of man as we know him, of that person that we are.

The person who enters ever more deeply into the vision of the crucified, in which evil becomes sin and sin becomes forgiveness, finds, in an ultimate mystery, his or her own identity. We know at last who we are. We know at last the being that we have dreaded and desired to be. We experience this identity as liberation from "the world," from the whole customary complex web of conspiracy that is its systematic denial. We cannot praise sufficiently the blood that that world has shed. We cling to the figure on the cross not with the desperation of one in search of a savior but with the passion with which we embrace the being that God calls us to.

The specific beauty of the crucified is the beauty of our human identity. In contrast, the whole life of historical man appears as typed: a human stereotype as opposed to the real being. In the man on the cross, I find an identity and a world to live it in, that my education and my gradual acceptance of it declared to be impossible. No poet has conveyed more vividly than Wordsworth the contrast between human promise and human fact, but Wordsworth's contrasted splendor is the innocence of childhood:

Heaven lies about us in our infancy:
Shades of the prison-house begin to close
Upon the growing Boy.

The true splendor is a transfiguration of evil with love.

In this vision, man of the city becomes man of the universe. The former's affair is with the institutions of his own creating. Only through the crucifixion of Jesus do we act out this ritualized denial of ultimate identity to the point where it becomes an affair with the universe beyond the city. For only faced with the good that we have destroyed because it is good, do we say, not to the city but to the stars, "this is what I am."

The mystic seeks an ultimate identity. Such a person is impelled forward by the inadequacy of all the city's answers to one's self-questioning. We may well see in the Christ-figure the powerful symbol of the self that we seek to become. If we are realistic, our Christ-figure will be crucified. But the only way in to this identity with the figure on the cross is via the sinfulness that has put him there. *This* dimension, of the confessed crucifier, is the vigor, the honest humanity, the political realism, of our commitment to an ultimate human identity and mission.

No hero figure can sustain the contemplation of being-hungry man, save the crucified. The Letter to the Hebrews states, "Without the shedding of blood there is no forgiveness of sins" (Heb 9:22). We have become accustomed to stop at the *exegesis* of that text, relating it only to a primitive world of religious discourse. Yet it is not that without blood God is not satisfied. It is that without blood our root evil is still in hiding, so that we are not yet prepared or able to hear God. In this context, Eucharistic Prayer III says, "see the Victim whose death has reconciled *us* to yourself." We need the blood, not God.

The bloodstained figure flashes back to us as betrayal what we otherwise experience as the ordinary and accepted limit on our potential. This is the foundational instance of consciousness-raising. In the crucified, we see the cost of identity, and the betrayal of it, and, in the love that we feel coming into us, the transformation of the betrayal into the paying of the price. This new exercise of the heart's affections changes the world on which we look out. We will forever return to question the crucified who has given to his immemorial involvement with ultimate reality the embarrassing, bewildering, and gloriously obvious character of sexual intimacy.

Finally, it is impossible to live with this mystery of the crucified as the symbol that transforms evil into sin and sin into forgiveness, without coming to see that this crucified embrace of God *anticipates* all evil, and the conscious creation that must carry the potential for evil, as well as *embracing* evil after it has become fact. The scholastic distinction between an "antecedent" will of God, that does not contain the cross, and a "consequent" will of God that does, misses the enormity of what the cross reveals of God. Christ's blood streams in the firmament of the beginning, as the sign of the universe it is to be, one, that is, whose hidden pitfalls themselves open onto the new fullness of being. The cross of Jesus, as sign of the power of love over evil, is appropriately placed at any point in space-time. It is trivial to regard the creation of potentially sinful man as "a risk that God took," with the cross of Jesus as the remedy God applied when the risk became disaster. Such an account fails to see the difference between saying that God is able to draw good out of evil and the more radical statement that God's love *embraces* evil. This is not to say that there is evil in God. It is to say that God is a reality in which evil is mysteriously transmuted. Not the philosopher's evil that is pure negation and easily seen to cancel out in God, but that evil which, short of God, is the most real thing with which we must deal and whose succumbing to God in our hearts will cost us and give us everything.

This *radical* statement about God and evil comes close to saying something about God, about his *character*. It suggests that God is prepared to *push* us into evil and beyond into the vision of the heart of being. Evil is not so much an obstacle that God can overcome, as a tool in his hands. As the symbol of *this* sort of God, a God we cannot get at *short* of evil and who therefore in some way wants us through evil (in the sense of wanting my son through law school!) the cross of Jesus is appropriately placed as the foundation of the created universe. And Revelation speaks of "the Lamb that was slaughtered" (Rev 13:8).

5

THE RECOGNITION OF JESUS

Jesus Christ, in the experience of the believer, is a man who lived two thousand years ago. But he is this man *recognized* as the expression, as the personality, of something in the soul or psyche of the believer as a human being.

What is this "something"? It is the person's life, sensed—however obscurely—as hungry for some ultimate meaning, convinced of some ultimate meaning. It is the root of rare moments of an unaccountable happiness. It is what all idealists and reformers draw upon. It is why there *are* idealists and reformers. It is a spark of the divine. It is what Augustine speaks of when he says, "Thou has made us for thyself, and our heart is restless till it rests in thee." "Our heart," in this statement, is "this something." God's destining us "for himself" is, however obscurely, *experienced* as restlessness, and, even more obscurely, as promise. There is promise in us. And this "promise" is a promise of life. It has to do, not with something we want to get, but with being ourselves without any inhibition. The greatest happiness possible, and the very definition of *happiness*, is to be oneself without any inhibition. Augustine is saying that we can only be this way "in God."

The recognition of Jesus as "this" is the work of the Holy Spirit in a person. The Spirit alone has the subtlety and closeness to the individual's life to awake, in response to the image of Jesus, his very own sense of desirable being, what *he* would give everything for. It is the Spirit that roots Jesus in the ongoing history of the individual. And while what the individual experiences, and "would give anything for," is simply "Jesus," the motif for this experience and love is being woven out of the most essential substance of the lover's soul. The saints whose profession of love for Jesus takes extravagant and sometimes embarrassing forms, are people who have allowed the Spirit to make conscious, to a degree far more than usual, this inner core of humanity within them, and to identify it with Jesus. In other words, the love for Jesus has, under the Spirit, a very strong subjective component: nor is it possible without this. Thus, Paul writes, "No one can say 'Jesus is Lord' except by the Holy Spirit" (1 Cor 12:3). It is not simply that the Spirit tells the believer that Jesus is Lord. The Spirit tells *this* believer what "Lord" means in his or her life.

But to say that this psychic marriage between Jesus and the believer's innermost reality is the work of the Spirit is not to deny to that marriage all other intelligibility. Something of the subjective component, of the human ideal, is spelled out in the traditional formulations of faith. Thus, for a people whose thirst for the fuller life crystalized in the figure of an eschatological Messiah-King, "Jesus the Christ" means, "Jesus the embodiment of our desire." Now, the name "Jesus Christ" as it is repeated countless times every day in the liturgies of the Christian world, *is no longer doing that job*—and that job needs to be done. Similarly, the important thing about calling Jesus the Logos is the intense human passion that was once crystallized in that expression. These titles, which originally linked the Jesus of history to the human psyche in its generation of human meanings, lost this force and became abstract theological titles locating him in a system of belief rather than in the psyche and experience of the person. As a result, people lost the capacity to see Jesus as the reflection of *their own* deepest lives, feelings, and aspirations.

Not only do those ancient titles no longer fire the soul of the believer, but we are now into the era of "psychological man": we are beginning to be in touch with that psychic center from where, in an earlier time, we naively projected an image of the consummated or ideal man—the Christ image for instance. This center Jung calls "the self." He means the obscurely perceived totality of a person's life as a reality able to become conscious and to be a source of psychic energy far in excess of and more far-reaching than the self of which we are readily and inescapably conscious and that we call ego. My life is so much more than me.

A new title for Jesus is beginning to form in people's lives. He is "the self." This title is basic to understanding Jesus and his saving passion that is worked out in this book.

This understanding of Jesus as "the self" is, in the primary sense, deeply traditional. It is carrying on the traditional and indispensable practice of relating Jesus to one's self-understanding. It is, in the terms set by "psychological man," making overt the subjective component in people's faith in Jesus. More precisely, it is doing what must be done for this subjective component around a shared and explicated belief. It remains true, of course, that only the Holy Spirit *makes* Jesus the transforming symbol of my innermost life, of the inward shape of my motivation. To cooperate in this making, I need self-knowledge—as the Christian mystical tradition has consistently maintained. I need to be pointed, and by the confident instruction of a shared faith, to that spacious country of myself that lies in the shadow of the ego, in order to experience its coming together in Jesus. I need also a vivid sense of my impatient and fearful ego-life as riding roughshod over that fine country, crucifying my "Lord of glory." I also need to experience this situation as, in recollection, the forgiveness situation, from where the energies of the new person spring.

To this end, I am developing this practice when I hear in the liturgy a text such as the following: "He has made known to us the mystery of his will, according to his good pleasure that he set forth in Christ, as a plan for the fullness of time, to gather up all things in him, things in heaven and things on earth" (Eph 1:9–10). I look inward and consider, when I hear the name "Christ," the vast inner resources of personhood and freedom and sacrifice that God is awakening in me as I fix before my eyes Jesus crucified. In other words, I consciously shift the center of gravity of the Pauline gratitude to God for Christ. That center has been "Christ, out there." Paradoxically, the more the Christian psyche has been disabled through a weakening of the Christian subjective component, the more it has fastened on the "Christ out there." To anyone conversant with psychology, this is not a paradox. The less we get from people and things outside us (owing to a failure within), the more we seek our weal just there. The mother-deprived person keeps going to the mother and her surrogates for life.

In John's Gospel, Jesus says, "Out of the believer's heart shall flow rivers of living water" (7:38). That is what it is to believe in Jesus. It is to have one's own floodgates opened. Into the image of Jesus on the cross—wood and nails and all—the psyche pours its endless and otherwise forgotten life.

6

SELF-DISCOVERY THROUGH THE IMAGE OF JESUS

I most deeply and accurately discover Jesus as the man I never was only when I realize that my not being wholly a man is what crucifies him. Jesus on the cross represents an identity that I am crucifying rather than entering. Yet my crucifying is my way of entry, for it represents my non-personhood forced into its characteristic action, which is the destruction of wholeness. So there I am, out in the open at last. But once out in the open, I lose the fight to keep what I *thought* was myself but was really my anonymity. Forced to hear myself saying, "I hate that which makes for life," I expose myself to sorrow, and sorrow, if I give it free rein, bears me in to the heart of the crucified where I discover myself. Thus, I am reborn in the identity that I have sought to fend off by crucifying. The way into this identity is the way of the spear: that is precisely why the crucified is the symbol of our lost and recovered identity. We crucify Jesus rather than be him, and thus, through the healing power of sorrow, we become him.

As I enter deeper into this mystery of blood and new birth, I see the sins of my past ever more clearly as expressions of *fear*. Fear was the point. Fear of that center where there is no fear, and as the center, discovered, shows up fear as hate, the fear thus exposed revives in memory as the heart of sin and the key to so much past behavior.

Only Christianity has the effrontery to *answer* the question, "What are we afraid of?" For Christianity, it is the least rhetorical of questions. At its center is the symbol that transmutes fear into hate and hate into sorrow and forgiveness. Or, in more generic terms, evil into sin and sin into sorrow and forgiveness.

If we concede that symbolism is the most powerful form of communication, and that a philosophy of man requires to find symbolic form if it is to touch us to the heart and move us, can it be doubted that the symbolism of the crucified is the most potent expression and resolution of the tragic drama of one's wrestle with oneself?

7

A NOTE ON THE CULT OF SUFFERING

One of the things that earns Christianity a bad name is the cult of suffering. How does Christianity clear itself of the charge, with its talk of desiring to be nailed to the cross with Christ?

It cannot, so long as it ignores the unique saving power of *Jesus'* suffering and the *way* we come to identify with the man on the cross. To understand the suffering of Jesus as the effect of my evil is to understand it as the suffering I am inflicting on my true self. Conversion, which operates through sorrow, consists in shifting my position from the crucifying ego to the crucified self. Jesus makes first conscious and then salvific the suffering that is inherent in our evil, alienated condition.

But if the suffering of Jesus is not seen as a place of self-discovery, if it is not seen as saving and the saving as self-discovery, then we find ourselves simply "identifying with a sufferer," choosing *him* as our hero because of some belief in the value of suffering.

Jesus, whose life reveals its meaning on the cross, is not for imitation. The agony in which his earthly life ends, while it is chosen by him and freely willed, is not chosen by him as a way of life but embraced by him as the necessary correlative of his sinlessness in a sin-world. *This* choice, which must be mysterious to us, is not like the choice to pursue virtue or wisdom—that is to say, not like the choices that we admire and try to imitate in our heroes. It would be a disastrous mistake to class Jesus' choice of suffering with Solomon's choice of wisdom. It would make a masochist of him and of his followers.

We do not follow in the footsteps of a sufferer; we find ourselves in the suffering that, understood as our infliction, resolves the evil in our condition. The reason why Jesus is not for imitation is not that he is beyond our scope or understanding, but that he is the identity of each of us.

8

THE UNHURRYING CHASE

Jesus on the cross frees man from that which puts him there. Who is "him?" Well, Jesus—but also that which Jesus represents, which is the wholeness of being human.

We need a new concept of this wholeness. We have considered humankind, and the evil within which sets us against the order in which we are called to truth and goodness and personhood. But this is not simply an order *in* which we are called wholly to be—it is the person we are called to be; it is our wholeness already known as his, as himself, beckoning to us, feared and crucified by us. It cannot be insisted enough that our evil is turned, in the deepest analysis, on us. In it, one hates *oneself* as the free being he or she knows oneself to be. One hates oneself free. This means, one hates oneself free from evil. One hates oneself free from sin. So, one hates oneself as he or she sees oneself in Jesus, the man free from sin. What Jesus shows is that there, where one should above all love oneself, is hate. This hate, *directly* opposed to our wholeness, as it only is in the drama of Jesus, succumbs to it in a new birth of the whole person in blood.

Thus, Jesus does not take us off the cross, but he frees us from putting ourselves there. Ever after, there appears in human life a distinction between suffering self-imposed through fear and suffering not thus self-imposed. The latter is the lot of the victims of the power hungry and manipulative. The former is the lot of the power hungry and manipulative.

One of the most important lessons we learn from the cross is that the wicked, the destroyers of lives and of life, are sufferers. The appeal Jesus on the cross makes to them is to see *themselves* as the victim of their malice.

The deepest and strongest peace a person can have is when he or she stops running away—when, that is, he or she *need* no longer run away, for it is a poor and nervous peace that one gains by merely forcing oneself to stop this flight. Peace is the cessation of a person's flight from oneself in the power of a new revelation.

What can *stop* this flight by rendering it unnecessary? The resolution of the fear that impels it. What a fantastic resolution of this fear takes place when, forced to turn into hate and crucify, it then succumbs to love! At ever greater depths of oneself, a person will see the bloodstained figure that contains the greatest peace that humanity can ever know: the peace that is the end of the otherwise endless logic of destruction that is the way of evil.

Here, we seem to have touched on another theme, that of nonviolence. A theology of nonviolence sees the redemptive action of Christ as consisting in a final, total because nonretaliatory, acceptance of violence, but this is not a separate theme. The fact that violence provokes retaliatory violence is only a special case of the general theorem that violence, until there is total resolution, must go on. A person in flight from oneself is intrinsically violent, and this violence *not only* provokes further violence but *itself* proceeds to ever fresh violence. The resolution in the Crucified is more radical than that which consists in nonretaliation. For it is the cessation of *that which provokes* retaliatory violence. Thus, a theology of nonviolence cannot afford the *principle* for a theology of redemption. It is itself derivative from the transformation of evil into sin and sin into love, which is the transforming symbolism of the Crucified.

Our self-hatred is not adequately expressed in the *interactive* process of violence provoking violence. It resides in the heart of the human that is the seat of evil. Our heart is not converted simply by seeing that the other to whom our violence is directed does not return it. Our heart is converted by seeing that one's violence is directed to oneself: to oneself dramatized in the symbol of Jesus crucified where he (man) appears as most lovable and most hated, and, in sorrow and pardon, most whole.

In sum, what the crucified Jesus is forever ending is not simply the otherwise endless process of violence provoking violence, but what powers this process, one's endless fear of oneself, one's endless flight from oneself, one's endless crucifixion by oneself. That which stops at the Crucified and so enters peace is more than can ever be seen working itself out between us: it is the unfreedom, in one's past and present, that is uncovered and cleared at ever greater depths of contemplation of Jesus making peace by the blood of his cross.

To invoke a powerful image from Ayn Rand, the symbol of Jesus crucified is addressed not simply to man the violent but to that deeper desperation that is driven to kill "in order not to let himself know that the death he desires is his own."

But it will be urged that the practice of nonretaliation does precisely what I am claiming that the Jesus-symbol does: it tells the destroyer that it is oneself that he or she is destroying.

It is true that the nonviolent response to violence throws the violent person back into him or herself. While the response is violent, the violent person feels justified, and can go on believing that his hate has an object other than himself. The other person is unwittingly cooperating in my game of saying that it's not me that I hate, not me that I fear, not me that I'm unhappy with. This applies also to the theorem of transference and countertransference. By "transference" I put my guilt, my self-hatred, into you. Once you pick this up and start reacting, once, that is, you unwittingly let my transference become in you a "counter-transference," you are backing me up in my flight-from-self. This means that reality, your reality, some reality other than myself, is backing me up in my flight-from-self. (Making you guilty and wretched *is* my flight-from-self in action. It is not merely the *consequence* of my flight. It *is* it. *You* are where I am running to from myself.) When you spot what is happening, and stop the countertransference, you cut off the corroboration you have been affording me. I am thrown back on myself and forced to carry on *in there* the business that I have been much more satisfactorily and satisfyingly carrying on *with you*. I founder. There is a horrendous description of this event in an extreme form at the end of *Atlas Shrugged* when the supreme phony, who has been applying electrical torture to the good man, suddenly realizes in this the whole of his life and past as a grotesque act of self-loathing.

But here there is no healing. On the one hand, the tortured man becomes for the torturer "a pretext that has totally broken down as a pretext," "an alibi that has driven out the wretch who sought shelter in it," "a moratorium on the inward hell that has expired, driving the torturer back into the inward hell." In our affair with the crucified, on the other hand, the tortured man becomes a *symbol* of the self, the beauty, of the torturer. The beautiful tortured body of Ayn Rand's hero says in effect to the torturer, "Take your dirty problem away from me, where it has no place, and bury it with yourself in the hell where you belong." The tortured body of Jesus says to the torturer, "I am yourself, your beauty, which you are crucifying." That is the specific nature and power of a symbol: the power of the other, of the not-me, to represent my wholeness to me. That is the essence of the believer's vision of Jesus crucified: that the tortured man shows to me my crucified wholeness in a way that is full of invitation and hope, a way that invites me, as into my home, into the self that I am crucifying.

Let's clarify this difference between these two torture situations. Once that power of the facts has surfaced, the Ayn Rand one illustrates the power to destroy the cheat. In the confrontation of the person with Jesus crucified, this same power of fact invites and does not repel. This *gathering* as opposed to *disintegrating* force of truth is what we call its symbolic communication. We define *symbolic communication* as the conveying of awful truth invitingly, but this is not a sugaring of the pill. The point is that the true symbol, the Jesus symbol, makes the unbearable truth of ourselves bearable through the power of love. It makes the center bearable not by disguising it but by attracting us into it. It puts the truth there for life, not for death.

By the *facts*, I am found out. By the *symbol*, I am found. Interesting, the expression "found out" implies that when the inspector called I was out! I was not on the spot. I was off-center. I was not in control. All these images refer to that falling short of personhood that is the essence of evil.

The *manner* of this invitation, of this attractive and leading way of saying "I am you though you will not see it," is, as noted, symbolic. But this word *symbolic*, here, only names the structure, the manner, the style, of the communication. Something immense is required to *make* and *empower* this symbol of the crucified in the citadel of the soul. That "something" is the historically reported goodness of Jesus, combined with the psyche's deepest power to project in symbol its drama of self-crucifixion, these two components fused in the power of the Holy Spirit, the spirit of wholeness.

There is another way of expressing this distinction between nonviolent response by itself and the full meaning of the crucified. To be changed, I need *not only* to be chased out of hating myself *in* another, *but also* brought to seeing the self, that I hate, *as* other, as a man abandoned on a cross. I need to say, "*There* is my life, my beauty, my possibility, my human- ness, my full experience as a human that is a personifying of the universe, my outrageously ignored and neglected dream of goodness." And *that* welcomes me. That *means* me. That is my meaning. That is my symbol. That is my sacrament. That is my baptism. That is my bread and wine. That is my love. The self that we hide in others to neglect and destroy it there, needs to be seen symbolically, whole-makingly, *as* another, before we can appropriate it. Its otherness is the spur to sorrow, which is the organ of its appropriation.

I am talking about the difference between two kinds of symbols. There is the personal symbol whereby I invest other people with my hopes, my ambitions, and my guilt. Then there is the great transpersonal symbol of the crucified whole, that draws for its power not on the desperate and diverse politics of our self-evasion but on the deepest resources of the psyche where it is touched by that power that creates and holds and promotes all being. The breaking down of our personally constructed symbols, in the undoing of our transferences, is indispensable to our growth as persons. But it is a fatal error to go to this demythologization for the model of the savior- encounter.

9

IS THERE ANY SORROW LIKE UNTO MY SORROW?

The mystery of the cross makes explicit the suffering that is implicit in the reign of sin. Just as it makes explicit, as sin—such as the clear Adamic sin redivivus—the evil that pervades human life: just as it dramatizes as an act of willful *destruction* of the whole person our habitual practical *negation* of the whole person, so this mystery features, in a fully explicit form, the *suffering* that this destruction inflicts.

This raises an extraordinarily delicate question. We have seen that it is only in the context of a person's encounter with the crucified in faith that this prodigious making-explicit of evil as sin takes place. Neither the members of the Sanhedrin, nor Pilate, nor the soldiers, performed *this* critical all-evil-expressing sin of humankind. Only a person who, faced with the crucified, is awakening to all his or her depths, sees in those depths, as the crucifying of the Christ, the evil that has pervaded all his or her life. But the question is this: If none of the *agents* in the drama performed this sin, did the man on the cross *suffer* it?

Certainly, there is in the encounter with the crucified, in which the archetypal potential of the psyche is stretched to the full, a mystery of concreteness, I dare to say, a smell of blood. Although it is myself that is coming alive in the encounter, although it is a self far wider and deeper than that of common experience that is coming into individuality as my own, nevertheless, there is, as an essential part of the encounter, a man, not myself, who suffers much.

There is something strange here. It might appear that "communion with an archetypal suffering Christ" and "historical recalling of a man who once suffered" are two perfectly distinct operations, neither one requiring the other. But these alternatives so understood do not fit the Christian contemplative experience. It is as though my recognition of myself in the suffering Christ, which is necessarily and consciously incomplete and progressive in nature, demands, as the corollary of this incompleteness and the support for this progress, that the portion of the Christ that I have *not* yet appropriated be concretely realized in someone, and not merely reside in the inexhaustible archetype. At every stage of my personal entry into the mystery, the Christ that I have *not* yet become is a man who somehow *is*, and not a platonic *anthropos*-image. This tension is essential to the encounter. Resolve it by dissolving the thought of the Jesus who was on that cross, and the encounter itself, with all its power to evoke in me the self, falls to pieces.

We can enlarge this picture. We have seen that the believer relates to Christ as part crucifier and part crucified, there being between these two an infinite number of gradations. In so far as I am not finding myself in the crucified, I am the penitent crucifier, and so I shall be, and so every believer will be, until death. In so far as I am the crucifier, the crucified is other, is not-I. And the only meaningful representation of this not-I is a real person, another human being. Make of *him* simply the as-of-yet unappropriated self, and the tension and realism of the encounter collapses. The suffering-of-sin that I have not yet found in myself and found myself in, is in a real body nailed to a cross.

In other words, while it is my true self that I progressively *discover* in the contemplation of the crucified, it is not "my true self" that I *explore* there. The field of exploration—that which underscores the exploration, is the man on the cross. And while it is perhaps impossible to say exactly what this means, the suffering in which man in his evil situation becomes critically explicit had to become explicit *first* in a man. That man must appear to me as one step ahead of me in the growth in identity that is mine in the encounter, and the identity in which he is ahead of me is not located merely in the indefinite potentiality of the archetype. It is nailed to a cross.

Supposing we took Bultmann's approach, conceding that there had to be *someone* called Jesus, upon whom the whole thing could be built up: that someone could be any pious person who suffered what is, after all, the fate of many pious people. Does that work? For me, absolutely not. The consciousness of Christian myth as having *that* sort of historic foundation does not make the encounter with Jesus crucified significantly more concrete than if the whole affair were frankly said to be no more than the negotiation of an archetype.

Of course, once we reject Bultmann's view, we create fresh problems. For are we not *then* committed to a historical Jesus who would consciously represent the passion of all humankind? I think that we have absolutely no means, no terms, for the positive description of the type of consciousness that would be capable of that suffering that the Christian mind and heart learns to have been the suffering of Jesus.

It is in this context that we appreciate the economy and adequacy—we might say the elegance—of the New Testament clue: the man without sin. This is a potent double negative, and a double negative communicates in a very peculiar way. What is "a man without sin" like? We don't know, in the ordinary way. I think that this phrase speaks best to—and is meant to speak to—the faithful encounter with the crucified. It describes, not genius or any known human excellence (except goodness, which, however, ultimately *is* an elusive quality), but only *that* individual human reality that the Christian soul intuits, in the manner I have suggested, as underlying and forever standing ahead of the encounter.

10

THE MEANING OF SIN

Since the main contention of this book is that the forgiveness of sin is the central idea of the New Testament, it is necessary to clarify the meaning of sin. There is an ambiguity in the concept of sin that creates untold confusion.

The two senses in the word *sin* are a defect that is predicated *of* the human condition, and a defect observed *within* the human condition, by some people in others, by some people in themselves, taking an enormous number of forms. The first sense has for its point of reference some order embracing the whole of reality and equated by the believer with the mind of God—in relation to this order it makes sense to say that "humankind" fails, resists, refuses. The second sense has for its point of reference the *human* order as expressed in this or that culture, with the possibility that we may find a few offenses recognized as such by all cultures—in this order, all offenses are judged in relation to the world of meanings constituted by humankind.

More simply, the first sense of sin relates it to a world of which humankind is *not* the center, while the second relates it to a world of which the human *is* the center.

The use of the one word in both these senses is as embarrassing as it would be if we had one word that sometimes meant "color" and at other times meant "red."

Clearing up this ambiguity may seem simple. For who will not be struck by the difference between humankind's "failure of the Universe" and an action like theft or murder or rape? And yet it is not so simple. For there is an overlap between the two meanings of sin. It would be morally insensitive to say that rape is ultimately sinful only in the sense that cathedrals are ultimately sinful, in other words, to *reserve* the ultimate meaning of sin for humanity's sense of oneself as the center of reality, a meaning no more or less verified in any one work of humankind than in any other. The human sense of self-centrality is *more clearly recognizable* in some attitudes and actions than in others, that is, in those attitudes and actions that society recognizes as bad. It being always understood that society has some huge blind spots, and that it is society that says to the individual to allow me "to take the speck out of [your] eye" (Matt 7:5) while ignoring the plank in its own.

What we must concentrate on, then, is not the attitude or act that is being described as sinful, but the *horizon of meaning* against which it is seen as sinful. Here, the distinction is clear. On the one horizon of meaning, rape is the action of a person choosing his or her own gratification despite the dignity of another, of him- or herself, and of the entire social order. On the other horizon, it is the action of a person choosing oneself as he or she immediately experiences oneself, against all possible and conceivable reality, against God.

But even here, a difficulty must be noticed. To confine ourselves to the "ultimate horizon" would be, for most of us, to weaken our moral sense. Imagine the fulminations of the prophets against extortion, oppression of the poor, and pride, deprived of the natural moral indignation of humankind as he contemplates the inequities within the human world. Nevertheless, this very fact that the thought of God is not enough for us as moral sensitizer demonstrates that "the thought of God" is incredibly weak in us, corresponding hardly at all to the flaming and all-consuming reality. This indeed is sin, in a meaning now very close to the one it is to have when we consider the forgiveness of sin in Christ. The theme of the gospel is that the "ultimate horizon" is becoming near, vivid, and, for those who become open to it, all-controlling. This is the reign of God. In this perspective, we can see what sin is: Sin is the unreality of God; sin is the unreality of the real to the unreal; sin is the unreality of life other than the small portion of it that one calls one's own and builds into immobility; sin is a monumental indifference to the totality of which one is a part and is otherwise without meaning. Once this is understood, certain things become clear. First, the forgiveness of sin, the unhardening of the heart, is the most urgently desirable grace, and will be central to any religion that takes both God and humankind seriously. Second, the more monstrous human evils such as the Nazi camps, easily seen by us to be evil, are cynically thorough applications of the sinful principle that is not so easily recognized. Third, these obvious and repulsive manifestations of our evil exemplify the sin for which Jesus dies, only when they are so understood. Fourth, the dramatic difference between these great evils and the way we decent people live, easily leads us to go to them for our *concept* of sin, and thus to see sin as the *aberration* from a human norm rather than as the *exaggeration* of a human tendency. Fifth, the idea of gross sin as aberration rather than exaggeration destroys our understanding of the doctrine that Jesus died for our sins.

I have said that the ultimate horizon or perspective does not obliterate the distinctions observed in the shorter perspective, nor does it equate the rapist with the cathedral builder. But the *reason* why it does not do this is all-important: one who understands sin in the ultimate perspective has no concern with the comparison of action with action, whether to pronounce them unequal *or whether to equate them*. He or she is overcome with the enormity of human self-centeredness in a universe of being whose center is God.

The person who awakens to this enormity in one's life

will, most likely, first do so in the context of those actions and attitudes that show up as sinful against the *nearer* horizon. The reason for this is that in such behavior I can more clearly hear myself saying "to hell with everything but me." Thus, the newly awakened Ignatius thought of his sexual promiscuity and daring. It takes considerable schooling in self-understanding to discover the "to hell with everything but me" that underlies the most innocent attitudes and actions. This may be the reason why the gospel prefers prostitutes to Pharisees. In a world where all are blind to the roots of behavior, the gross sinner has a more colorful past in which he may see more clearly the choice of self against God. The Pharisee has a spiritual subtlety that will stand him in good stead once the conversion process has begun, but that is liable to prevent its getting started at all.

The convert's recognition of his sinfulness in the context of "near horizon" sins also contributes to the confusion between sin in its two horizons. The depravity of Ignatius and Augustine, so well intended as an encouragement not to despair of the mercy of God, has the effect of disguising from us in what that mercy consists: the awakening of a person from that deep sleep of which the grosser sins are but the nightmarish activation. Even the attitude of Jesus to prostitutes becomes counterproductive for theology. Presented as showing God's merciful approach to sinners, it conveys the assumption that "prostitutes, for instance" are what "sinners" *means*. It isn't.

None of the complexities in this question of sin must be allowed to obscure or qualify the fact that when it is *redemption* from sin that we are considering, when it is that forgiveness that God gives in Christ, and especially when we say that the forgiveness of sin is the heart of the New Testament, we are referring exclusively to human behavior seen against the "ultimate horizon," where its enormity consists in the Godlike status that the human implicitly claims in all that he or she does and makes.

Conversely, where there is no realistic and convincing *notion* of this "ultimate horizon" meaning of sin—of this sin *of man* as distinct from the sins of men—the mystery of the Redemption is bound to become a dead letter. If what Christ saves us from is not some perceptibly awful fate, what is this salvation worth?

Here, however, we must make a distinction. Just as the Holy Spirit reveals Jesus to a person as his center and true life, even when Christology is floundering, so the Holy Spirit instructs the faithful heart in the radical meaning of sin, even when the theology of salvation is confused. But when it is a question of getting this theology clear, we must seek a radical idea of sin not only in Spirit-directed meditation but in a generally available human self-understanding.

Such self-understanding is becoming available. With the cumulative loosening of cultural assumptions, it is becoming possible to see the whole human project from the outside as a necessary denial of an equally undeniable contingency, and so to see our entire history as characterized by this denial. Until this perspectival shift, the sin for which Christ died is no longer what it had to be, namely, a refusal of "humankind" in respect of God, *symbolized* in the myth of Adam, and *somehow* present and operative in human history. That "somehow," filled in by rhetorical descriptions of the human scene in which all human evils, from greed to death, were jumbled together, can now be replaced by a clear idea. Evil is operative in us as the denial of our contingency through fear, and as the cognate fascination with ourselves. It is the inescapable narcissism of consciousness. It is the denial of a contingency that finds its full acceptance only in Jesus on the cross, where sin puts him and must put him.

Thus, the myth of Adam, out of which the Christian tradition of self-understanding has spun its yarn, becomes wedded to the myth of Narcissus, in which the psychoanalytic tradition of self-understanding has seen the human trauma as it unfolds. As the narcissistic interpretation of humankind breaks, with Becker, onto the ontological level, it pairs with the myth of Adam: the myth of Adam showing the price of *becoming* conscious, the Narcissus myth showing how that price is paid.

Fascinatingly, the root of human evil as finally laid bare in a *secular* tradition of self-understanding yields a theory that is astonishingly like the Christian idea of sin. Let me explain this similarity. The denial of contingency explains at one and the same time the "normal" and the "abnormal" in human behavior. For the "normal" are those who achieve a relatively successful and socially accepted denial of contingency, while all the aberrations and perversions classified by psychoanalysis are so many bizarre and unlivable solutions. One basic formula—the denial of contingency—affords, at once, a better understanding of the "abnormal" forms. It does not merge the normal and the abnormal. On the contrary, a grasp of the root human evasion highlights how very *differently* different conditions of people do it. And this is not at all unlike the Christian idea of sin, which illuminates simultaneously the consciousness of the decent person and the monstrous forms that sin can take. Note that I am not equating the monstrous sins with the psychological perversions. I am pointing to a significant similarity *of pattern*. As the perversions stand to normality in a world where *all* are denying the basic human truth, so the more glaring sins stand to the decent person in a world where all are denying to God his total reality. To the new psychological perspective, in which we are all, in a sense, mad, there corresponds the Christian perspective, in which we are all sinners.

The new perspective, in which secular man sees himself as born into a life-problem that far exceeds the limits of ordinary self-awareness and is therefore a problem that is theological in all but *name*, is of the greatest significance for theology; theology, which, for its part, has leaned too heavily on the *name* of the God who creates, questions, and draws us, rather than on the experience of being created, questioned, and drawn.

11

INTENSIFYING THE VISION

Through the Christ-event the wrestle of man with his God-intended self is dramatized and led through the phases of rejection, hatred, crucifixion, destruction, surrender, and new life. Oscar Wilde said, "Each man kills the thing he loves." Those who stop short of evil in themselves will never know what love is about. They will never receive the crucified.

It is not for nothing, on the contrary it is in exact conformity with an exact law of the psyche, that the symbol in which evil is crystallized to the eternal renewal of life, could not be bettered as a symbol of humankind's futility. A body left to bleed to death on a cross. Death at its most eloquently indifferent to all that we believe in. All this is in order. In the all-sustaining power of God, evil has been allowed to express its triumph over humankind in a total symbol: a symbol whose totality is its undoing. The crucifixion of Jesus is the symbol in which evil tries to hold its own against God, and thus provokes the thunder of resurrection.

What I have, in the sight of Jesus on the cross, is not the *motive* for believing in God's love so that this belief will *then* overcome my self-hatred, but the actual *process*—made visible, dramatized in the flesh—whereby my self-hatred reaches its climax of realization, avowal, confession, and surrender. One's self-hatred is not only the *obstacle* to one's acceptance of God's love. It is the *medium* in which God's love is revealed

47

to us as it transforms it. I meet God's love not by turning away from the hatred of myself to another motif, but as a climax of my self-hatred, its crisis and resolution. God does not just give me a *reason* not to hate myself. He transforms my self-hatred into love. That is the meaning of the cross.

Once we realize that our sin *is* self-hatred, it becomes clear that Jesus, representing our self, suffers our sin. The suffering of Jesus is the suffering that is the passive component in our sinful condition: it is that suffering, of our true self at the expense of the ego, that receives its full, symbolic, resolving expression in the crucifixion of Jesus where it receives the noble name of passion.

In the mystery of Jesus, contemplated in faith, the sinful human plunges, murderously, desperately, hopefully—who knows?—into the self with which he has ever been at odds, and there is accepted, there finds identity and freedom.

A powerful recentering of this mystery of love and blood is achieved once we acknowledge that sin is in its essence self-hatred; the more self-hatred that shows itself in a person, the stronger the touch of God becomes for that person. Yet for *this* proposition to qualify for theological acceptance, the "self" must be the viceroy of God, a worthy *human* object of the sin that offends *him*. That is why the main probe of a reunified soteriology must be an energetic and imaginative grappling with the sort of thing that Jung meant by "the self."

The standard account is less than incarnational. It secures the incarnation *first*, as God's identity with Jesus, and *then* has Jesus on the cross, expressing God's love. It does not dream of the awesome fact that God's love has become incarnate in a process that resolves the flesh's enmity with itself as his creation.

12

THE INESCAPABLE RHETORIC OF PERSONALITY

As we grow older, we become more sensitive to our interaction with other people. A huge fact begins to dawn on us: that no one is, or can be, neutral. Often, it is the very people who persuade us by their openness and honesty who, when we are removed from their company, make us wonder, "Was not the inattention they managed to create in us toward the more petty and sordid side of life, itself a deception?" I think particularly of the good, beautiful, generous wife of a suspicious, unlovable husband—a deeply wronged woman surely. Yet there may be terrible cruelty in the nonexistence for her, which she communicates to me, of the things that loom so large in her jealous husband's eyes.

When someone is trying to persuade me how deeply he or she has been wronged, there is always one vital thing left out: the other person. He may constantly refer to her with genuine desire for understanding her point of view. However, another person's point of view is, essentially, the other person: not anything that he or she may be *understood* to be claiming, but by their very existence, the claim that they *are* on life.

Each of us makes a case for oneself, but each of us *is* a case. No one's case, in that sense, gets or can get the consideration it deserves. The reason why the person from whom I seek this consideration cannot give it is his concern with *his own* case, and *that* is the one thing he cannot get consideration from *me* for! So that which withholds another from considering me is that which I cannot consider in him. That part in me that leaves you alone in your tragedy is my tragedy. This is not a picture of universal selfishness. It is simply a picture of selves together.

Each person is, of his nature, a magnetic field that distorts reality into its pattern. Each of us wants, and must want, reality to be after the manner of his field. There is an appropriate loss of innocence that comes to see that, while the manipulation of others in its grosser and more cynical forms is to be deplored and curbed, a person-with-others is manipulative by nature. Each of us wants it our way. To cease altogether so to want it is to cease to be a person.

Yet I am also dissatisfied with having it my way. I experience that in *thus* having it my way I am not free. Language expresses this fact. For the tone of voice in which one says to a person "have it your own way!" is a tone that *withholds* something. Verbally, it gives freedom; in truth, it withholds it. The most dishonest statements are those in which we give each other freedom. Permissive statements are dismissive statements.

What we more deeply seek from each other is another kind of permission: a permission to be myself, that is not simply a concession to my magnetic field, that does not consist in drawing an invisible ring around me and agreeing, inaudibly, not to encroach. Within that ring, I have no freedom. The only *climate* in which my freedom can flower is the climate that is constituted by, and consists of, other selves. What we call a community is a being-together of people in which the *very thing* that imposed caution on my claim for myself and led me to lie to the other people about my claim—that is, other people with *their* claims—has managed somehow to become the climate, the warmth and moisture and sunlight, in which I live and make creative and self-revealing initiatives. Such extraordinary human phenomena exist, but they are rare.

The reason they are rare is that most people cannot afford them. I cannot afford to let you be yourself, to the extent that I cannot afford to relax *my* hold on reality, to turn off my magnetic field, to rid myself of that inner fear whose outward face is disapproval.

But this is not as simple as it sounds to some people. It is no problem at all to the hippie, who turns off the current with the utmost ease. There is in this person no potential disapproval. *Anything* you do will meet with an open smile. This, of course, is a cheat, and the person in you knows it. If anything goes, then you are part of "anything." The hippie does not say, with the bourgeois, "Leave me alone and I'll leave you alone." He says, "What's all this talk of leaving alone? There is no alone!" And there is. It is bloody. It is hideously hungry. It is vulnerable. Its name is "human." Thinking to make a climate for it, the hippie makes a desert. It has been said by some who have experienced it that there is nothing quite so palpably empty as a place that the hippie community has left. San Francisco was like that when they moved on. This fever of instant love transformed our complicated species into a swarm of locusts.

The process whereby a person is transformed from the passionate hold on reality that he natively is into being a holding-ground for others, from merely *seeking*, to *being*, the bread of life, cannot be short-circuited.

I need to learn that my hold not only impedes your quest for life, but also impedes my own, as yours impedes yours. Correspondingly, it is not only your way of living that paralyzes my self-expression and says, "Don't risk it!" My self-expression is impeded by *my* hold on reality. At the center of the turmoil, in other words, is the person in turmoil with oneself. More specifically, it is what seems and must seem to me my thrust for freedom, my drive to live, that is the structure of my unfreedom. My hold on life is a stranglehold. Can I release it?

It is at this point that Christianity makes a most extraordinary and ambitious statement. Initially, it says, "No, you can't, and stay a person. Your hold will relax only when you go through a total change." But even that is easily said: it will be taken to refer simply to the *magnitude* of the operation. What is outlandish about Christianity is what it says of the *manner* of the operation.

For the operation consists in taking this self-destroying stance of man and arranging for it to *go much further*. It creates for the feared, ill-known, and repressed self a symbol—a symbol not taken simply from the world of dreams where it certainly acquires its symbolic status, but from the very history in which the person hacks out his way; a symbol that, once it has shown itself as the very heart of the human, calls forth *all* the fear that is in humanity in the act of its destruction. More importantly, this showing is not, primarily, for one's *rebuke*. It is for one's acting out. It is designed to let him or her destroy one's wholeness and *so* to discover the love that is the indestructability of that wholeness. Only in the power of a love stronger than oneself in his passionate hold on being, can one live the community of humankind. One comes under that power *only* by shooting one's bolt, by exhausting one's power for an ultimate and Godless selfhood.

The Christian is a person who has shot his bolt as a person and found oneself twice a person in the love of God. The identity that slowly flows into us as we learn to live with the crucified, is the life that, while it properly bears our name, is the climate in which others are finding their growing.

Now this operation is of a wonderful psychological exactitude. Psychology has come to understand the value of the ego. While the study of depth psychology, unfolding as it did the riches that lie in the unconscious, was tempted to see as its task the weakening of the ego in favor of this superior source of life, a more mature and practiced understanding has shown this policy to be disastrous. Somehow, the power of the unconscious must be invoked in a manner that does not introduce doubt and wavering into the ego.

Now, if I am asked to name a mystic exercise in which the ego would have full scope, I cannot think of a more dramatic example than the contemplation of Jesus crucified. For in that contemplation, my ego becomes conscious of itself as the crucifier. It is no serene paradigm of human wholeness that is placed before me for my dreamy meditation, but the victim of the way I live. Mysterious though it is and must be, the process whereby a person enters more deeply into life as a necessary and forgiven crucifier of life, answers, to an incomparable degree, to the requirement of depth psychology: that the ego undergo transformation yet maintain its proper vigor.

13

CONCUPISCENCE

In every major decision, there is, underlying the clear question as to which course to pursue, the obscure question, "What sort of person do I want to become?" The underlying question, for all its obscurity, points to the nature of freedom. At critical moments, especially when one unbosoms to a close friend, the underlying question shows itself: we have an acute sense that that is what is at stake, and that that is *why* this decision is momentous. But this question is never without obscurity; nor does it ever describe a situation that we can totally master. That kind of description refers, naturally, to the clarities of the first question: Shall I take the job? *There* I am, in the ordinary understanding, free. But at the deeper level of the second question, my freedom is never that clear, and this is precisely where my freedom is most real, most present, and most itself. This is the central paradox of freedom: where it is most itself, it is, to a considerable extent, unrealized. Where my freedom most truly is, is where it is only *trying* to happen.

It is trying to happen, trying to be, *in* that ongoing process that is my life. That thrust goes ahead inexorably, however conscious or unconscious we may be in it. I am a complex and, in a sense, well-run household, a complex of systems dedicated to my survival. It is well-run in that it will keep going, somehow, in whatever circumstances. Karl Rahner calls this my "spontaneity." By "concupiscence," he means this spontaneity *in so far as* it is working on its own and not as the implementation of my freedom. It works thus on its own to a considerable extent in all of us, to a markedly lesser extent in a holy, whole person, but still to a significant extent in all men and women.

How does this concupiscence relate to evil? It is not itself a proneness to evil. Evil is not *in* my concupiscence, by the fact that it is not with my freedom but going its own way. Evil, in other words, is the lack of wholeness, of all-togetherness. It consists in the fact that my freedom is confined to the sphere of my decisions, of whether I take that job or not: my freedom in taking the job does not realize itself much at the deeper level at which the question, "What sort of person do I want to become?" poses itself. In taking that job, I will, in fact, be defining to a further extent the sort of person I am becoming. But how much do I have to do with that becoming? How much do I carve myself in the job that carves me? *That* is what is meant by the question, "How free am I?"

We might clarify this by distinguishing between "my freedom in decision" and "my freedom *under* the decision." In so far as my freedom in decision does not penetrate to the level of my spontaneity, we have the "concupiscent" situation. I am free in respect of the job, unfree in respect of myself—and, as I have said, it is there that I most need to be free and that freedom really *is* freedom.

Evil, I repeat, is not *in* my spontaneity but in the out-of-phaseness of my spontaneity with my freedom in decision. Being out of phase, *neither* is necessarily better or worse than the other. *Either* may be on the side of the angels. Thus, if my spontaneity is heading toward a destructive relationship, my decision to go against my spontaneity and not enter the relationship will be the right decision, and in this case, it is my decision-part that is on the side of the angels. Yet on the other hand, I might, in an important matter, decide to lie. In the act of lying, I blush violently and give myself away. In *this* case, it is my spontaneity that is on the right side, but in neither of these two cases do we have integral goodness. We have only a partial attainment of the good: in one case, by my decision, with my spontaneity left out in the cold (and please God it will *get* cold!); in the other case, by my spontaneity, with my decision-part exposed to shame. The *radical* evil in these two situations lies not in my spontaneous proneness to adultery but in the fact that my *avoidance* of adultery is not with my whole being; not in my deliberate lie but in the fact that I *can* act with only part of myself.

Luther says that all men are disobedient to the Law of God, because the Law of God requires obedience from the heart, and a "concupiscent" person *cannot* give obedience (a decision) from the heart (one's total spontaneity).

This is the meaning of Paul's statement in Romans, that "the law is spiritual; but I am of the flesh" (Rom 7:14). *Spiritual* means "addressed to the whole person," "requiring obedience from the heart." *Flesh* means "not *being* a whole person." The human divided cannot respond adequately to God who requires the human whole. Thus, it is a misunderstanding of this text to say that the part of a person that *can* obey, the decision-part, is the good and spiritual part, the spontaneity that doesn't go along with this obedience is the bad and unspiritual part. There is no "good *part*" of a person, for good is of the whole: it is in non-togetherness of the parts that the evil of humanity consists.

God seeks from us, as alone appropriate, the movement of his whole being, his life. In other words, he seeks our praise.

Thus, we must think of integrity or human wholeness as that condition in which the sphere of personal choice, more precisely of self-disposal, is coextensive with and is expressed in the world of a person's natural movements and spontaneities. A condition for which, in Jungian terms, there is no more "unconscious." Such a condition is not the human condition as we know it, although it consists in the harmony of two parts of the human that are clearly meant to be in harmony. When they come into a partial harmony in a person, all but the perversely unpeaceful recognize in that person the figure of the wise and desirable man.

Now traditional scholastic theology claimed a very surprising thing about the state of freedom from concupiscence. Although the state of nonfreedom was obviously a sickness, an unwholeness—with the implication that the cognate wholeness would be a "natural perfection"—traditional theology said that freedom from concupiscence was a preternatural gift of God, not a perfection of the kind that the Creator "owes" to the creature by reason of the latter's divine essence. In other words, it conceived of the human person as by nature sick!

I suspect that this idea was an inspired guess. The dividedness of the human person between self-disposing "person" and spontaneous "nature" is the most radical one we know. The varieties of its dialectic are endless. Its power to queer the pitch in human relations is likewise endless. By this analysis, we are light-years beyond the picture of the human person as having a "good" side that tends to God and an "evil" side that tends away from God.

Consider the case of a person who freely decides to seek and to do God's will but who encounters violent opposition to this decision in the sphere of his or her spontaneous desires. Now, the customary simplistic analysis of this situation says that the above description *is* its analysis, with the will for God, concupiscence against him. These spontaneous desires not only militate against the free decision for God but make that decision the poorer and the less Godly by their absence from the dominion of the will. The temptation I must resist contains a vital element of the goodness in whose name I resist it.

I recently described my life as "divided between men in search of life and half-men in search of God." That is a rather vivid description of the state that is not free of concupiscence: not free, that is, of the great human separation of powers, of will and appetite. This separation appears equally in my pious friends whose pursuit of God leaves out so much of human appetite, and in my impious ones whose appetites forever postpone that discipline in which alone they can flower and improve the human condition.

I have spoken earlier of our resisting the fullness of personhood to which God is calling us. I have depicted Jesus as the symbol of this wholeness, and of his crucifixion as the bringing out into the open of our resistance to becoming whole. Now, what Rahner has pinpointed is the *structure* of man's refusal. The refusal of God's call to wholeness is the tendency of decision and spontaneity to stay apart. We prefer them apart. Faced with any decision, we strive to leave part of ourselves out of it. We resist a temptation, but we keep it going. We make a decision, but we look for the escape clause. Nothing is final in this life—and by God we want it that way. We are inveterate two-timers. I absolutely dread the thought of the whole of me coming together in a yes to somebody or something, with nothing of myself left out, and therefore no possibility of retreat. Yes, I *want* it, too, I know. Sometimes I feel for it in prayer, but the dread and the desire are inextricably intertwined.

14

REAL REDEMPTION

Christianity is revolutionary. It makes the death of Christ reconciliatory in the sense of making *God* convincing to *us*, of displacing for us the God of our fear. It makes it clear that it is *only* a question of opening *our minds and hearts* for God to appear. No question of placating *God*. It refers to the miraculous cessation of fear, and the consequent appearance of a totally new God, no longer the God we have seen filtered through the human nightmare.

This revision, however, requires prolonged and sustained meditation, to appreciate fully how much is involved in our approach to religion and to its connection with our human relations and how much of our natural and customary religious thinking goes in the direction of placating *God*. It will be worthwhile to make this overt at various levels.

First, at the level of formal theology, theologians affirm that there is no question of placating God in the literal sense, as in pagan sacrifices, but there is a mass of conflicting theories regarding how the propitiatory sacrifice of Christ works. The whole thing is said to be "mysterious," which, in the context of clearing God of bloodthirsty sentiments, makes us suspicious. We have a right to expect a clear statement as to why this sacrifice is not a placating of God, namely, that it is a placating, a pacifying, *of us* about God or to let God in. In the usual theological account, *the direction* of the movement *from us to*

God remains unchanged, with the vague qualification that the normal function of a bloody sacrifice is somehow modified. In fact, the point that theologians describe as mysterious is embarrassingly simple—like the sudden discovery that a person who appears to be behaving in a most extraordinary way is in fact in love with me.

Second, at the ethical level, we call upon the experience that tells us that the arrival at truth is a painful and costing affair—the passion of Christ is a striking example of this. Our model is Pelagian, making of the agony of Christ the supreme example of "getting there at the cost of blood." Once again, the *direction* in which we are thinking is "from us to God." Jesus "made it"—for us of course, though how this act of monumental stoicism is "for us" remains unclear.

Third, at the more primitive level, which is still potently operative in us, we think of religion as a series of attempts to win God's favor, the sacrifice of Christ goes into a practical osmosis with all the dodges we use to this end. Once again, the direction is "from us to God," and is a matter of "us getting there."

Now this direction, which is presupposed at all these levels—intellectual, moral, and primitive—*is reversed*. Not modified, not substituted for by some *other* way, not *getting further* than the pagan sacrifices, but reversed.

Once this direction has been thrown into reverse, we begin to think of God in a new way. We need to think of a God closer to our evil than we ever dare to be. We need to think of him not as standing at the end of the way we take when we run *away* from our evil in the search for good, but as taking hold of us *in* our evil, at the sore point that the whole idealistic thrust of humankind is concerned to avoid.

Let us now ask *why* the spontaneous and inertial direction of our thought is "from us to God." The answer, already implied, is that the conscious animal is impelled *away* from its center as a being at once self-aware and at the mercy of total process, to fashion an ideal, a projection, an ennobled existence able to forget its frightening contingency. *All* that it dreams up in this desperate enterprise, all its institutions, all its symbols, all its power-figures, all its gods, *even its image of the one God*, are functions of this great movement *away* from the center *toward* the ideal. Thus, the religious quest, whether we view it in the propitiatory sacrifice of the Incas or in the intellectual and moral strivings of Plotinus, is "trying to get there," "trying to make it." The religious dream is the dream of humankind's self-ennobling, of our achievement of meaning, as at last "coming of." When, through the Mosaic and subsequent revelation, there is engrafted into this dream a belief in the one God who is transcendent, and when, finally, we learn that union with this transcendent Being has been achieved through the death of the Son of Man, millennia of psychic habit in us hear this as meaning that at last the transcendent God has looked down and said, "Okay, you made it, I am satisfied." Redemption through the blood of Christ is interpreted as the bending of Reality itself to man's great dream of himself.

Yet, it is exactly the reverse. It is the ending of the dream. It is the beautiful collapse of the whole enterprise. It is the invasion of man by himself, with God at the center as love.

All this sounds theoretical, but its import is embarrassingly practical. For the implication is, that just in so far as our religious mind is operating normally, God's making of love on the cross should appear to us as pathetic. It *is* pathetic. It is *in* the pathetic. It is in the unbearable place.

For the person who seeks it in the place of his nobility, his sublimity, the Absolute is in the pathetic. The revelation of God's love in the passion of Christ is far more like the embarrassing and happy discovery that someone is simply in love with us than our mind is *capable* of reconciling with the way we still *have* to think of God. Those moments of revelation between two people are temporary and blessed reversals in man's flight from himself. The cross of Jesus, looked at with faith, is the total and final reversal.

But this total and final reversal takes place in the context of the people we are, still conscious animals scared of our animality and seeking to ennoble ourselves. Still only able to survive in this way. In other words, there is a tension here that will only be resolved in the Parousia. This means that our normal humanity, with all its interpreted experience, is always in the position of being surprised by the humble, pathetic, and kind of ordinary nature of God's love in Christ. Meditation is a discipline that each of us must discover in the way most suited to him or her, for increasing the frequency of these moments of surprise. A Jesuit retreat director created one of these moments by pointing to the crucifix and saying, "What a way to run a universe!" The vision of the crucified is a huge therapeutic interruption of the struggle to survive. St. Paul writes, "In Christ God was reconciling the world to himself" (2 Cor 5:19). Try, in this text, to hear God saying, "I am in the Man you are destroying in your search for me."

In William Shakespeare's play *A Comedy of Errors*, each character is mistaken as to the other characters' identity and intentions. In the denouement, all is discovered to the happiness of all. Our entire religious history is a comedy of errors. Its denouement is on Calvary, but this denouement takes place at the heart of a still darkened world. It is for the empowering of saints with the laughter that will in the end save the world.

15

A PRECISION

"You contradict yourself," someone will say, "for at one time you speak of man as self-crucifying, at another as self-loving, self-worshipping, self-absorbed."

What we are trying to look at is "humankind without God," the most powerful self-contradiction there can be.

Of course, we are never without God. In Christ, we are *with* God so wholly that this condition demands for its full understanding a correspondingly rigorous idea of humankind without God. The Christian fact generates, of necessity, the possibility of its absence. It is in the nature of a master switch that, thrown, would plunge the world into a fearsome darkness.

Looking, then, at the *logic* of "humankind without God," we see the human person saying to one's life, "You're all I've got"—and do we not know from experience what a threat to the beloved lurks in that style of love-profession? In fact, this act of self-worship sets the limitless miracle of the human person's life on a pedestal, where it becomes limited, a possession, an asset. So, the underside of the worship of humanity is its paralyzing, its immobilizing. The inner meaning of self-worship is self-crucifixion.

Part Two

THE DEAD AND RISEN

1

EVEN UNTO DEATH

So far, we have considered only the dynamic of *the crucifixion*, and we have concentrated on this dynamic as it happens in the experience of the believer. Now the death of Jesus *as a process he undergoes* has not entered into the building up of the dynamic. The dynamic is one of confrontation, consciousness raising, sorrow, healing, and self-discovery. Central to this dynamic is the death of Jesus *as caused by sin*, but not the death of Jesus *as a process he undergoes.* That is the *extension* of the dynamic, not a primary ingredient in it.

This distinction is vital. This book can be summed up in one sentence: His death caused by sin is our life. His death caused by sin is salvation. The confrontation between man the sinner and Jesus crucified is how salvation happens. The mistake is to miss or blur this foundational idea, and then to speak of Jesus' death *as a process* that is, in prototype, the salvation of man. This is the mistake of putting, in the place of the victim who mediates the forgiveness of sin, the hero who, in our name, breaks through death to new life.

Jesus does break the power of death for us. But the *power* of death—as opposed to the *fact* of death—is due to sin, and so Jesus breaks this power by mediating the forgiveness of sin. There simply is no other way to break it.

Given this, the death of Jesus as process becomes meaningful. The death of Jesus can then *only* appear as process, and not as the enigma and tragedy that death in our world is. What I now want to say depends wholly on getting this order right: *first*, sin and its resolution; *then*, the symbolism of death.

Why did we get this order wrong? Why did we get fed up with the sin-business and meditating on Jesus on the cross? For myself, I lacked the maturity to see sin as self-crucifixion. I did not have anything in my psyche to *see* in Jesus on the cross. I think that's why, having had that experience in the Italian church, I promptly forgot it.

The evil preference for unwholeness is the desire for death. Preeminently, it is the desire for the death of Jesus who represents the whole man.

But "evil desirous of the death of Jesus" is evil on the verge of redemption. This is the ultimate mystery of us: that even our evil, even our tendency against wholeness, exposes us to the love of God. It exposes us to that love in a way and at a depth to which even our desire for wholeness does not expose us. This is the psychological reason for the dogmatically cliched statement that only by the blood of Jesus are we saved, only by his stripes are we healed. Jung insists that evil has to enter into our integration, and charges Christianity with leaving it out. Jung is right about evil. It has to enter. In an unfathomable way it *desires* its own transformation. But evil enters into the total transformation only through crucifying Jesus.

Note

It is only in a world in which freedom and spontaneity have become synonymous that the redeemed condition would be adequately *defined* as one of freedom. That is not the world of our experience. Thus, the "freedom" of the new creation may only be hinted at. It is conveyed through image and symbol rather than conceptually. The mysterious thing about this freedom is, that it is *at once*, and in one miraculous and total transformation, the freeing of will from the enslavement of desire and the freeing of desire from its enslavement by will.

2

THE DEATH OF THE LORD

What a fuss we make about death! The way we think about death is the extreme case of the ego's habit of characterizing a larger reality, of which it is part, by its effect on itself. "Fog in the Channel. Continent Isolated," a nineteenth-century English headline read. If we could be observed by some being from outer space who was perfectly integrated into the life process, he would say, "These humans regard their reentry into the life cycle exclusively as an event happening to *them*. They seem to have some *other* thing going for them than life, and they understand death not as part of the life process but as the cessation *of that other thing*. Thus, they speak of the death of their great men as though it were a great misfortune, a turn of ill luck, that should not have happened. It is very difficult to convey what *they* mean by 'death.'"

We turn away from our animal involvement in the life process, and throw our best energies into doing those things that with death will simply cease. We have our ego, and then death has its, and *its* is the last word. Thus, we confer on death the quality of victory, a quality it does not have of itself. As though the water were to say, on reaching what *we* see simply as boiling point, "the fire has conquered." Instead of being a moment in the process, death for us is the breakdown of the attempt to live eternally and in despite of the process. Since the attempt to live eternally and to constitute reality for ourselves is that arrogation of divinity that is called sin, death for us is the penalty of sin.

Furthermore, death regarded in this way is an isolated event. It is the end of your thing. It is the end of my thing. There is nothing so isolated as the way in which each person tries to center the world on himself, tries to constitute his own reality. In other words, there is nothing so isolated as what our galactic observer sees each human as doing "besides living," of which *we* see death as the ending. Correspondingly, there is nothing so alone as the death that terminates each man's "thing that he does."

And so, death—viewed from the standpoint of the ego— has two qualities. It is the victory over meaning as we try to secure it, and it is an isolated event. These two are complementary, for the absolutely isolated event is by definition the event without meaning.

Another effect of the ego-perspective is that death becomes as it were personified. What for the galactic observer is simply the point of reentry into the cosmic process is for the human the Great Event. Our ego-operations are so important that what brings them to an end is correspondingly important. It is a Thing in its own right. "It" triumphs when in fact all that has happened is the reentry of an animal into the life process. Of the universal process in which things come to be and pass back into the process, the humans have their peculiar version, according to which *I* manage to get something done and then "Death" triumphs. Thus, the reification of death reflects the illusory centrality of the ego.

Now, in Jesus, we honor the man without sin, the man without private building. In contemplating his death, we are forced to see human death in its primary meaning, as reentry into the process.

But because Jesus is not a *regression* to the innocent animal state but an *advance* into further consciousness, this purely processive nature of death, which he realizes through sinlessness, is a "return to the Father." The symbolism of return to the Father is heavy with meaning and healing beauty. It is experienced by us as a huge deculturalization of death, a lifting of its heavy somber symbolism, a cleansing.

But how are we, children of culture, to appropriate this new symbolism of death? Death for us remains laden with its human meaning. How can we celebrate this primary death? For symbolism is not changed by an act of understanding. Symbolism is only changed by a radical shift in experience.

Remember that it is sin that confers on death its *old* symbolism. Sin is the constituting of our own reality as *the* reality, making of death the ultimate victory. Now we have seen, in the figure of the Crucified, the destruction of our larger reality made overt for us, and thus overt, toppling over into the all-embracing love of God. We have experienced, in this vision of the Crucified, the forgiveness of our sin, and *thus* we are liberated from the old, sinful vision of death and enabled to see our victim in his death as "returning to the Father." The Father whose infinite embrace receives us sinners receives in that same embrace, and as the focus of our new vision, our bleeding victim. In acknowledging ourselves as sinners, we find our identity in the man our sin has crucified, and in him, know death as the Father's embrace.

That is why our Paschal liturgy constantly invokes, for the validity of its great image of the Lord's passage to the Father, the resolution of our sin in the crucifixion. That is why the Hero of the Exsultet is he who "by his holy blood paid Adam's and our debt."

I have said that death, understood within the limits of culture, is a meaningless, isolated event. At the opposite pole is the death of Jesus, which is universal in scope, being what death, regardless of culture, is for humankind. Yet we come into this universal scope only through the forgiveness of our sin, because it is our sin that makes death the ruler and will continue to do so until it has found its resolution in the love of God.

This bears out one of our main convictions here: the anthropology of the New Testament, of the new man, only falls into place when it is centered on the forgiveness of sin, more precisely, centered on the Crucified, the mirror image of sin, which offers forgiveness to those who look into it.

This also means, conversely, that to appropriate fully and celebrate our condition of forgiven people we need to exercise ourselves in the contrast between the death of Jesus as a liturgical fact and death as our culture mourns it, for this contrast is the full symbolic extension of the contrast between the regenerate and the unregenerate condition. As a theme for meditation, ask yourself, what sort of a funeral would you give Jesus? Have some fun with this. How about a slap-up affair, with gun carriages and a gun salute? Then you might suddenly realize what an extraordinary man you've got on your hands and in your heart. The medieval Church got close to the gun carriage when it celebrated Good Friday *in black*; a deviation itself oddly instructive.

We are thinking of that cultural misfit, a death that *means* "return to the Father." One of the things our theology most needs is a tightening up on the handling of symbolism. For how many theologians and spiritual writers, for instance, is not Jesus' self-oblation on a cross simply the exemplar of the "holy death"? The category invoked is "death as we know it but made by a holy person the occasion for the ultimate act of surrender to God." *In* that category, Jesus is supreme. The *symbolism* of death remains unchanged. Whereas, in truth, the symbolism of death is here broken open. This is the meaning of "dying you destroyed our death." *Our* "death." What we have made death into. He who contemplates the death of the Lord enters a new world, or, rather, he enters the hitherto unexplored depth of *this* world, in the penetrating power of the Spirit. And therefore, the death of Jesus is a theme for celebration independently of the Eucharist that is its celebration. The Eucharist *grows out of* the death of the Lord, implementing the latter's inherently celebratory character.

3

THE END OF THE JOURNEY IN SIGHT

The real meaning of Jesus' death is one purely of consummation.

Now this "meaning of consummation" is, at one and the same time, the clearing of death of its heavy cultural symbolism, its ego-centered tragic quality, and the full flowering of the victim in his power to absorb and transform our evil. As the full development of the victim, his death takes us deeper into the forgiveness experience, since this latter is the subjective component in our vision of the victim. Thus Jesus, in his transformation of "our death," perfects in us the forgiveness experience. The believer's eyes are opened to a world unclouded by culture-qualified, ego-centered death *not* through some cosmic ideology but through the experience of forgiveness in its completed state. It is the deep, labyrinthine, complex, and evil-complicated heart of man that must be opened for the new world to appear. The cosmic Christ, the Christ that death liberates, is the Christ who conveys the message of forgiveness to the depths of the human heart and so makes it cosmic, not just civic. It is *as* this finality of forgiveness and divine presence that he *appears* "in the glory of God the Father."

To the believer, to man-in-forgiveness, this death is *joyful*, in a human world in which death cannot be wholly joyful.

Finally, this death is *glorious* with the glory of another world, the real world of God.

Thus, while scriptural exegesis distinguishes two great themes or motifs of redemption, namely, expiation and passage out of this world to the Father, these are only two dimensions of one Christian experience. Endlessly they interpenetrate. For the way beyond this world—this human culture-defined world—to the Father is the way of forgiveness. The victim who awakens and accuses sin and resolves it in forgiveness, the person who decentralizes death and makes it a passage beyond this world, and the son who is in the glory of the Father, are one and the same symbol, mediating one same experience of liberation.

As the victim dies and changes "our death," we see further into the victim out of a deeper experience of forgiveness; in seeing him in his end, in the glory of the Father, we know the complete form of that experience.

As sin in us has "our death" as its full extension, so precisely does sin's victim have a death that is return to the Father as *his* full extension. As "our death" is the perfect symbol of sin in us, so the consummated victim is the perfect symbol of our forgiveness. As the school of humanistic introspection teaches us to see further and further into our death out of further and further reaches of our futility, so the school of the cross teaches us to see further and further into the victim out of further and further reaches of our forgiveness.

The unity of the two redemptive themes, of expiation and passage, is the heart of an integral Christian experience. Jesus does not take us to the Father by going on that journey as our representative and carrying us along with him by throwing out sacramental lifelines. Jesus goes to the Father in our experience of him as victim, which is our experience of ourselves as forgiven and cut loose from our self-made world. "I am ascending to my Father and your Father, to my God and your

God" (John 20:17). His exaltation as victim, completing as it does the forgiveness of our sin-captive and culture-bounded heart, puts us at last in the liberated condition in which God can *be* God. The passionate and total experience of God as Father, which makes Jesus the victim of narcissistic and fearful humankind, is given to us in the forgiveness that the victim mediates.

It is seriously misguided, then, to advocate a shift of emphasis from the "old-fashioned" Jesus-on-the-cross-for-sin approach to the "more positive" theme of the Paschal Mystery, the passage of Jesus to the Father. "The Paschal Mystery" being the full development of the mystery of sin and forgiveness through the victim, a failure to grasp the latter will be enlarged in the picture we form of the Paschal Mystery. This picture will be a hotchpotch of myth and cheery optimism: an even worse insult to the heart than the dreary old meditations on the passion.

With the contemplation of Jesus *dead* on the cross, our journey into the crucifix comes to its end. While "Jesus crucified" has raised the issue of sin and dictated the dynamic of salvation, "Jesus dead" raises the issue of sin's anthropological extension, "our death," and dictates the full extension of the above dynamic into a new anthropology with death as passage and God as God. This final vision of the crucified is the Trinitarian theophany. The Holy Spirit in this theophany is the fully extended subjective dimension upon which the objective vision of the victim and his glory in the Father increasingly depends. The Holy Spirit weds the man on the cross to the forgotten and emergent self of the believer, and thus enables us to see our salvation in a joyful and cosmic death into the glory of God the Father.

4

JESUS JOINS THE FATHER IN THE HEART OF THE BELIEVER

The expression "perfect conformity to the will of God" is the overwhelmingly preferred description of "Christian perfection." It means a loving acceptance of whatever God may send, and that "whatever" can be genuinely open-ended. It thus includes "death, accepted purely as the will of God."

What it gives no hint of, however, is that even the human person with Christ, insofar as one thinks of oneself naturally and still has to think of oneself as living in this human world, *is not capable* of accepting death "purely as the will of God." Such death is "our death"—the tragic and enigmatic downfall of the anti-god, of the ego-centered consciousness. It is the enemy.

Thus, the spiritual axiom of total conformity to the will of God has to *presuppose* that massive transformation of death by Christ that is the central Christian mystery. Mysteries are not meant to be presupposed. They must be named, to school the mind and heart, and to be celebrated. Only in the context of this faith, contemplation and celebration, and as a comment on it, is the axiom of perfect conformity to God's will adequate to the new life. It is either a paschal axiom, or it is inadequate to the new condition.

It is not understood as such by spiritual writers. For the tendency is for it to create its own mental world, thus generating as the symbol of perfection the image of a human person, within the world as we experience and interpret it, totally accepting the will of God. Thus, Christ appears merely as the most perfect example of this type of obedience.

In reality, his is that unique obedience to which death is not "our death" but the gift of the Father. "Death as the Father's gift, as the Father's love in action" is the prerogative of Christ. It is only by assimilation to him through the forgiveness of the depth of our being, that it is ours.

However, we cannot speak of assimilation to Christ without considering him as he is now. His present condition is implied in the fact that his death "destroys our death." In other words, the corollary of "dying you destroyed our death" is "dead you are not among our dead." Let us examine this proposition.

There is an immediate and necessary connection between the way we, in our self-alienated condition, see death, and the way we think of the dead. *Think* is not an adequate word. It is rather a question of the way the human psyche experiences the dead. This is reflected in all the great literature in which the psyche finds expression, and in all the great myths of man.

Remember our galactic observer. He said, "These humans see death not as a moment in a process, understood in reference to the process, but as the solemn end of something they have temporarily snatched from the process."

It might be thought that the dead would exist for us no more. What happens is almost the contrary. Our sense of death, which we repress when we think of ourselves, our life, and its opportunities, finds its outlet in the way we view the dead.

The death that we will not allow to have *any* hold on us, we see as having a *total* hold on the dead. All the unknowness in life, that militates against our ego-centered building, we invest in the dead. We cannot bear to think of *ourselves* as but part of the total mystery, so we think of *them* in this way. They are the alibi for our sense of death.

This constitutes a deep divide, a gulf, between the living and the dead: between the living who are *without* mystery and the dead who are *saturated* with it.

This divide, carried to its extreme, becomes meaninglessness. For then the dead are defined as "not living" and the living defined as "not dead."

We are moved away from this extreme by poets like Rainer Maria Rilke and the later D. H. Lawrence, who raise up the dead as the accusers of our shallowness. In James Joyce's short story *The Dead*, the not-so-young bride recalls a long-dead young lover on one of the first nights of her marriage. Although the relationship was not a serious one, the husband feels it would be an intrusion to sleep with her. Going to the window and looking out at the falling snow, he feels *all* the dead rising against him, accusing from nameless depths the vulgarity of his ego.

It is not only these works of literature that tend to topple our safe view of ourselves and of the dead "in their place." Ira Progoff says that people he has treated have had most fruitful dialogues with dead parents, and I have proved this in my own experience.

Nevertheless, the divide that we make between the living and the dead, though open to criticism and partial correction, is as incorrigible as sin; and, like sin, it looks not to *correction* but to *redemption*, a radical transformation. Indeed, even our more significant and more human experience of the dead tends to emphasize in its way the divide. There is a solemnity about the dialogue that smacks of our self-centered, humorless, Godless condition.

In blazing contrast with our world of the dead—with

our Sheol, our Hades, our stances, our shades—is the fact that Jesus, whose death exposes and invalidates "our death," *is therefore not among our dead.*

Of course, the statement "Christ is risen" is up for grabs. You can have him stepping out of the tomb. You can have him stepping out of whatever Sheol or Hades you locate the dead, or you can understand the statement in a "purely spiritual" sense to refer to the abiding truth of his message. But the most radical understanding contrasts Christ's condition with what the dead are for sinful man.

We can make the following rule for New Testament interpretation, in this matter of the Resurrection. That interpretation of "the Lord is risen" is closest to the heart of the New Testament that understands it as flowing most immediately out of his conquest of sin. As the fullest understanding of our plight is that we are sinners, so the fullest understanding of the Redeemer in his completed condition is that which sees this as the full radiation of his overcoming sin. Thus, "risen from the dead" means "not among our dead as they are for us sinners."

Of course, there is a linguistic difficulty here. For "risen from the dead" means that he *was* dead and then ceased to be dead. Yet could not the initial resurrection experience be the change *of the disciples* from experiencing him as dead to experiencing him as not among the dead? This would mean that the resurrection experience was their changing from the condition of sinners into the new condition of the redeemed. This is what the resurrection experience has been in the Church and its liturgy ever since. It is the total experience of release from sin. We see, in the New Testament itself, the progressive deepening of the interpretation: starting at "an event that happened to Jesus after he was dead," we arrive at the Johannine picture of resurrection as the direct emanation of Christ's salvific nature.

The image of Jesus burns in the soul of the believer with a fire that burns up his underworld, the extended creation of his pathetic self-sufficiency.

In our dead we see the life that we try to *ignore* and forever *postpone*. We see the mystery that we *evade*. In Jesus, on the other hand, we see this mysterious wholeness *not* as we evade it but as we *crucify* it. We see it, in other words, in the most radical form of our dialogue with it, the drama of sin and its forgiveness. Thus, in Jesus the mysterious wholeness of our life comes upon us and engulfs us with an immediacy that the dead cannot have. That in us which banishes the dead cannot banish him who undermines it.

We cannot receive from the dead him whose death never placed him there but speaks to our sin as its dissolution along with our death. Jesus is a mystery of total consciousness in which the dead fall away and are drawn into the new totality.

We have had him and we have him, too close to the center of our being, ever to lose him in death. We have had him, and we have him, thus close, because in him we crucify our self, are at issue with our self, and can find resolution only in forgiveness. This vast mystery of forgiveness binds into one the world of man that sin has broken into the two worlds of the living and the dead. How can we honor him who reunites all the worlds, if we will persist in a theology that still tinkers with those worlds and leads its Redeemer through their labyrinthine and man-made ways?

We should meditate persistently on the difference between "a victory of the life that we deny" and "a return from the life that we have lost."

We should ask ourselves what we are to make of a death that is not the denial of a life that is the denial of death! What makes all this so confusing and generates such a morass of semantic problems about "life" and "death," is the presence of the Father! With this death, he is here. This death is him here.

How can the death that brings the Father allow any problem to arise as to where the Son has gone?

The trouble is that we have no language for a human life that does not deny death. I mean, we can have no *word* for it, no *image* of it. Yet this is the reality that comes upon us in Christ. We negotiate it as best we can, and the best we can is to work out of our radical diagnosis of ourselves as sinners.

Note

It may help to set the foregoing ideas in a more overtly psychological pattern.

The psyche of the human person contains, or internalizes, all reality. It has its heaven, its earth, and its underworld. Its earth is peopled by the people we know. Its underworld is peopled by the dead. Its heaven is peopled by heroes—the "great dead"—and angels.

However, the psyche also has a *center*. The full task of the ego, which naturally thinks of itself as the center, is to come into full appeasement with the center.

Now the center, *by its position*, is alive to, and coordinates, the three worlds of heaven, earth, and underworld. Thus, he who represents or symbolizes the center, Jesus Christ, belongs to all three worlds—of earth, of underworld, and of heaven—*but by being the center*. Thus, he is not *located* in any—the earth, heaven, or the world of the dead. It is on this basis that we say that he is "not among the dead." He "knows," "has tasted" death, but by reason of his centrality. It is thus that the converted ego begins to know and to experience him—not in any of the psyche's worlds but at its center, and as its essential life.

But if we are to understand the nature of this converted experience of the center, we must ask *how* the ego comes into it.

The answer of the gospel has two components. On the one hand, it maintains that the center is not only that which coordinates the worlds, but is the place of *transcendence*, of surrender to the infinite power that contains and transcends all that is or can ever be. On the other hand, and just *because* of this pressure of the infinite, the gospel's way of human centering is mysterious, crucial, and humanly demanding. Thus, the gospel sees the drama of the ego's relationship to the center as a drama of crucifixion, sorrow, and forgiveness. *This* drama of centering *is* the opening of the center to the infinite. Forgiveness is the power of the infinite pouring in to the center.

Now we can bring together the meaning of Jesus as the center, "not among the dead," and the mystery of crucifixion, sorrow, and forgiveness, and say that Jesus is not among the dead. Jesus is *thus* experienced by the converted ego, *because* he has been really experienced as center *in the mystery of crucifixion and forgiveness*.

Finally, the center *thus* known opens to the infinite. Jesus, dead but not among the dead, is with the Father. The mystery of crucifixion and forgiveness, that alone draws the ego definitively to the center where Jesus is experienced as filling all the worlds and not *among* "the living" or "the dead" or "the great dead," opens out to the infinite.

Hence the scandalous simplicity of the gospel. Jesus can say "if you have forgiven your brother from the heart, you are with the Father forever. The whole mystery of the cross is active in you" (cf. Matt 18:35).

5

NARCISSUS MAN

In *The Denial of Death*, Ernest Becker writes, "One of the key concepts for understanding man's urge to heroism is the idea of narcissism. As Erich Fromm has so well reminded us, this idea is one of Freud's great and lasting contributions. Freud discovered that each of us repeats the tragedy of the mythical Greek Narcissus: we are hopelessly absorbed with ourselves."

This self-absorption is to the degree of "hopelessness." An immediate intuition knows that it is fatal. This intuition finds its welcome expression in the Narcissus myth. But to let the myth speak fully in us, it is necessary to do all we can to appreciate, apart from the myth and before we sail into it, the logic that ties self-absorption to self-extinction.

What then is the logical connection between self-absorption and death?

In the first place, self-absorption is the movement of the flight from death. It is the huge desperate choice, by consciousness, of itself alone as against the surrounding world that threatens to absorb it. Our self-absorption is our choice of self-awareness as against our animality. It is the desperate and unavoidable choice of only one of the two poles of our existence. So, self-absorption is the flight from death. Where one flees from death is into oneself.

But in thus choosing oneself alone, he or she is opting for an ultimate solitude. This choice can be made not only by the individual as the unconscious structure of one's desperation, but also by the whole human race. It *is* being made by the whole human race, as between the two poles, taking seriously only our self-awareness, ignoring our being-part-of, that is the ecology in whose balance we are partly animals. Humanity believes it can continue with all its Narcissistic human normalities, of war, of politics, of religion, and that somehow the vast *other* side of the picture will look after itself. So, in opting for "oneself as conscious," the human person is opting for an ultimate solitude.

The ultimate solitude is death. It is to be cut off from the tree of life, and to wither. Thus, by a paradox that is built into the nature of conscious being, one realizes as spiritual isolation what is in any case one's lot as animal. In the very flight from death, we reinforce its hold upon us, making of it a spiritual hold. Our flight from death accentuates it by making for ourselves a spiritual version of it. Whereas nature merely decrees death as part of her personal process, her bizarre creature chooses death under the more awesome description: alone forever.

This is what is meant by the scripture's description of the human person as "under the shadow of death" (cf. Psalm 23). It does not mean "knowing we will die" but "what we *do* and *become* under this knowledge." It is not to our mortality, our animality, that scripture offers a remedy. It is to the death that we become in our self-absorption. It is to what we allow death to become in us by fleeing from it in the hopeless pride of man.

Finally, some images from Eliot, to our purpose:

Those who sharpen the tooth of the dog, meaning
   Death
Those who glitter with the glory of the humming-
   bird, meaning Death

Those who sit in the sty of contentment, meaning
    Death
Those who suffer the ecstasy of the animals,
    meaning Death

—From the poem, *Marina*

6

INTENSIFYING THE VISION AGAIN

In Jesus on the cross, I see the man I dare not be, dying the death that I dare not die. Rather than be him, I kill him. But my attempt to eliminate him confronts me with the perfect symbol of the death that I fear to die.

Jesus enfleshes for me the identity, the personhood, that I fear. Acting out this fear, and killing him, I confront myself with the very reason for my fear; the death that I dare not die.

The awful secret is that "the man I dare not be" and "the death I dare not die" are one and the same thing. My violent reaction to the first only confronts me with the second.

There is an indissoluble connection at the heart of our being, between death and the real person. Yet so hugely resistant are we to this connection, so wholly built is our culture, layer on layer, on its denial, that our only way into it is through destroying, in the name of all our culture, and of our whole human habit, the real person. We thus create the symbol of the very thing we attempt to deny, the symbol of man consummated in death.

The cross is not the negation of culture. The cross is culture's negation of God, of total truth, of total reality, this negation seen in a healing symbol. The only redemption of consciousness lies in the discovery that at the limit of its claim to constitute the absolute world it creates the symbol of what that claim denies: man perfected in death.

The cross is the one totally realistic dialogue between the human person God made us and the human person we make ourselves. The realism of the dialogue demands violence—the full operation of man's resistance—and its victim. It is our victim, and he alone, who opens us to the death in which we are to find ourselves. There is too much in us that resists total truth, for us to come into that truth except via our resistance. The mystic who flies in to this center, must there look upon him whom he has pierced. He *has* pierced him, if he's a man, if he's concorporate with the human world. Remember the Christian tradition that says that I killed him, that my sins nailed him to the cross.

The cross is not God's denial of this world. It is this world's denial of God, the symbol of this denial that is the symbol of God's acceptance of this world. God so loved the world that he sent his only son. Any ascetical doctrine that sees in the cross the symbol of contempt for the world is a perversion of Christianity. For all its thoroughness in self-denial, it avoids that *central* self-denial that identifies with the crucifying world and allows God to show to us his sin and God's forgiveness. It assumes prematurely the stance of God, and so never meets him in his mystery of love.

Part Three

IN PRACTICE

1

SORROW IS ESCHATOLOGICAL

What is the essence of sorrow? In the first place, it relates to evil or harm done, whether consciously or unconsciously. Furthermore, while common sense wants to know how a person can be expected to be sorry for something he did not know he was inflicting, reflection shows that coming to know what one has been unknowingly doing to someone is *closer* to the essence of sorrow. I am speaking of the peculiar unconsciousness that is always an ingredient in human relations and that turns out to have been *itself* the infliction on another person, not merely that which *allowed* the inflictor to cause pain.

Furthermore, sorrow is different from regret. For true sorrow requires total acceptance of the new state of affairs revealed when I become conscious of what I have been doing. It requires that I live, wholly and without distraction, with the person I now see myself to be. Regret, however human and even inescapable, contains an element of playing the whole sequence through again in my mind, this time without the offense. Thus, a *part* of my heart is trying to keep its inno-cence, like Conrad's Jim, in *Lord Jim*, repeatedly acting out in his imagination those fatal moments during which he made that cowardly leap into the lifeboat, *this* time *not* leaping, *not* being the coward he now knew himself to be.

A third characteristic of sorrow is that it can only come to full stature when the offended person is wholly forgiving. A person who is wholly sorry is, to a degree far beyond the normal, self-exposed. For such self-exposure to be met with "well, we'll say no more about it," is degrading. A person who is wholly sorry is, by that fact, on for a dangerously new degree of intimacy. For this to be met by the other person out of the perfunctory resources of the earlier relationship, is for the primary human offense, that of being unconscious, to shift from the offending to the offended person. It is a terrible thing to exact as payment what is being freely given out of a broken heart, thus showing oneself unworthy of the penitence of one's friends. However, the undivided forgiveness called for by undivided sorrow has more in it of the divine than of the human. To err is human, to forgive divine. It is significant that William Shakespeare, in his most mature play, turns to the theme of forgiveness, *and* that he makes his merciful character a quasi-divine figure.

What lies at the heart of this sorrow, that sees evil in a past experienced as innocent, that would not undo that past, and that needs for its climate an unreserved forgiveness? What is this sorrow that is not so much *over* the past as *of* the present? What is this sorrow that is an awakening of the heart, yet has for its appropriate symbol the broken heart? What is this *change* of heart that is rather the *discovery* of the heart?

This sorrow is an awakening; that is, an enlargement of the present and a new promise for the future. Yet the past, while it does not call the penitent *back* to itself, is essential. Imagine David's tears before Nathan without an intense reliving of his treatment of Uriah the Hittite. The thing to hold onto here is the concept of the past's *reviving* in the present.

How then are we to represent the three dimensions of

past, present, and future, as they interrelate in the coming of sorrow?

Contrast this process with our normal passage out of the past, in the present, and into the future. Of the normal passage we are largely unconscious. We know the past as a situation that no longer prevails or applies, the present as a new call on our energies, and the future as the vague direction of our desire. Whereas in the process we are analyzing, the past is turning into the present, and the present opening upon a real and significant future, *in the consciousness of the person*. The *person* is growing, and *that* is his experience of time. He *is* a becoming. An innocent and unconscious past *is becoming* a conscious present that asks what is now the work of love.

This leads us to the crucial question. In this awakening of a once-unconscious evil to itself, in what is that evil now seen to have consisted? There is only one possible answer. My past evil is seen as my *suppression* of the self, of the true center, that is now awakening. Not you my friend, and not God, but my true self, is the victim of what I now know as sin. I hurt you, yes. I failed God, yes. But more radically than this and by a secret action that is the mystery of evil at its core, I rendered unable for you, unabundant toward you, and impervious to the voice of the Spirit and of life, that center, that heart, whence alone human goodness can come.

It is my heart that my friend wants and that God calls upon. A colloquial description is content to say that evil consists in *not giving* my heart, but the mystery of iniquity is that I may easily, and without infringing any commandment but rather allowing myself to be a decent average representative of my society, make it to be the case that I do not have a heart to give.

Scripture refers to sin as hardness of heart. But we need to ask *how* we harden our hearts. The trouble is that we confine our analysis to the human refusal in its practical effects—

the gift refused, the attention not given—and so do not attend to the hardening of the heart. So, we say that the sinner *has* a hard heart. His center, we say, *has become* hard. Thus, we fail to see the subtler point that the center as such cannot be hard. It can only be suppressed or, to change the metaphor, encased. We get so used to regarding the hard heart as *the source* of evil actions that we become incapable of seeing that the heart is the evil person's *victim*.

Now to the analysis of sin and its coming into sorrow, there corresponds that deepest analysis that is the center of the New Testament. At least, a correspondence appears once we allow ourselves—with more theological tradition behind us than might at first appear—to see in Jesus the symbol of the true self. Jesus is, most intimately and without the aid of any vague pious rhetoric, the victim of sin, because he is the symbol of the true self, of that which we allow evil in us to neglect, ignore, and crush. His is the heart that I have refused to myself, to you, and to God.

I believe that a new hermeneutic of the doctrine of the Sacred Heart would surprise us. It would show the unimaginable extent to which evil, in God's perspective, is *our* crucifixion. It could well be that the revelation to Margaret Mary was prophetic of, looked forward to, a newly internal understanding of theology. The vision is of an *inward* betrayal, and an inward healing: of the divine heart that man must eventually recognize as his own, wounded by the normal cultured life of man. This sorrow is the pangs of new birth. The essential pain of this new birth is indivisibly the pain in the heart of Christ and in the hearts of his awakening members. That which a person *becomes* in Christ is that which he *destroyed* in Christ: his ultimate identity, his freedom for God, his true self.

At the level of symbolism, there is a "family likeness," a suggested connection—suppressed at the cost of maiming the symbolism—between the piercing of Christ's heart with the spear and the "compunction of the heart" that is central to Christian mystical tradition. Compunction of the heart is more than the *resultant* of contemplating the heart of Christ. It is the entering into that contemplation, the *becoming* of what is *seen*, the putting-on of the crucified, the patterning-on the crucified. There is a middle term that holds together the piercing of Christ's heart and the allowing *my* heart to be "pierced": that term is sin's piercing of my heart, become a consciously appropriated act. The faithful vision of Christ's heart pierced allows me to experience my heart as sin's victim and as taking to itself the penitent ego in a new life.

It is not pious consideration that breaks the sinner's heart. It is his vision of it broken by sin and awakening to new life as the breaking action is appropriated. What lies at the heart of this vision of the Sacred Heart is nothing less than the ultimate confrontation, essential to Paul's Epistle to the Romans, between "sin," the universal, culture-shaping non-personhood, and "life," the life that God sowed on this planet with the birth of consciousness and looked to for his undivided praise and glory. The theater of that confrontation is the heart of man, finding at last its true reflection in the Crucified.

The strongest theological minds have avoided this vision, relegating it to the pious, who see the Sacred Heart as human only in the sense of being God's way of bringing home to us the enormity of sin as offense against *God*. It enables us to see sin as hurting God, but God is all truth. The way God brings a truth home to us is itself the truth. What is brought home to us by the vision of the Sacred Heart is that sin offends God by destroying us, and that sin is redeemed in our resurrection.

St. Bernard says that the most mature love is to love oneself for God. It follows that the most mature form of sorrow is sorrow over the unique life that I have made unavailable for the Spirit and for my brother and sister. *Such* sorrow is, indivisibly, the awakening of that unique life to God and to God's world of people. It is the tears through which we come anew to our God, to our husband and wife, to our friends, to life. Since it is in Christ that a person becomes mature to God and to one's world, it must follow that Christ *is* that life that one has killed and repents of killing.

A further step, hinted at already, is to say that unconsciousness not only *permits* sin but *is* sin. It is far clearer that it is *I* that am the victim of my unconsciousness than that I am the victim of what my unconsciousness has allowed me to do. That to which the crucified holds up the mirror is that in our normal living that has no place for, and sees no need to find a place for, our unique, hungry, humanity. It is that which will ask, "When was it that we saw you hungry?" (Matt 25:44). And of what will a person more innocently and self-righteously ask that question than of one's own neglected life? The crucified enables me to see the self I destroy in the self I neglect. He enables me to see that to neglect *is* to destroy. Thus, I come before the crucified *as a nonperson*, seeking to be awoken to the person I am. From him I learn that at my most innocent I am death-dealing. I come to him to learn the vertiginous leap from the person I have made of myself into the person I have in this self-making destroyed. Indeed, the reason why theology has become so myopic is that we have lost the blazing contrast between the God-made person and man-made person. We no longer hear, as pointing to the forgotten reaches of ourselves, "Behold the Man!" We have very little sense of as lost, that which the Son of Man came to seek and to save. We do not recognize him dying on the hill.

Nevertheless, what the Christian tradition has failed to see *intensively* in a single vision, it has *assembled*, piece by piece. It is in no doubt that the man born at Calvary is an unimaginably new man, his climate not the man-made city of historical man but the new eon of God. But it has failed to realize that the roots of this new way of being human must lie buried within the person we think we are. Thus, it has failed to appreciate that the crucifixion that is the threshold between the two worlds is that which crucifies, by its very normality and self-acceptance in a man-made universe, the heart that God has made and looks to for his praise and glory: our own. In considering the passage from the old world to the new, theology tends to look at Jesus' death not as *inflicted* but simply as the passage from one world to another that death may easily be thought of as being. I often find myself asking, wouldn't this theology work just as well if Jesus had died, with heroic patience, of lung cancer?

The turning point is sorrow. This sorrow, standing as it does between two worlds of human, the old and the new, is of more-than-human over less-than-human. It is of the more-than-human who appropriates all the evil in the world that makes us less than human, that crucifies in us the Lord of the coming glory.

In sum, that which makes of Christian sorrow an eschatological reality, the hinge between human-time and God-time, is the unity between the piercing of the heart of Christ and the compunction of our heart.

2

THE BUDDHA
AND THE CHRIST

Siddhārtha Gautama, who became the Buddha, came to think that desire is the cause of all suffering. Therefore, eliminate desire and you will come to peace.

This analysis does not go to the root of the matter. The cause of our unpeace and unfreedom is not desire by itself but desire mixed with fear.

Desire is basic. To be alive is to desire, but no sooner is desire conceived than fear says, "Where will you be if you don't get what you want?" A marriage is thus formed between desire and fear. It seems a natural, even an inevitable, partnership. For what more natural spur to desire could there be than the fear of not getting what I want? But the fear of not getting something is a motivation quite different from its desirability.

Normally we don't notice this difference. Desire, as we experience it, is clandestinely married to fear, very often even *directed* by fear. I spoke of fear as a *spur* to desire. Desire is the horse, fear the rider that has gotten onto its back. The horse is a good horse and, liberated from this dark rider, will bound for the heart of the sun.

Let me give some examples of this confusion of desire by fear. A woman can make a man think he is in love with her—and vice versa—by making him jealous of somebody else.

What is happening in the experience of the victim? "Something I might miss" has, imperceptibly, become "something I want." The most potent advertising involves this same manipulation of desire through fear. The center of persuasion is not the desirable object—the automobile, the aftershave—but "you *without* these things, you are bereft, you are impoverished." It is not appetite but ego that is the target of the advertising industry.

In these instances, we can spot the connivance of fear with desire, the self-insinuation of fear into desire, but experience teaches that only the Holy Spirit can bring us to that deep place in ourselves where fear and desire combine and dissolve this enslaving marriage. Even the Buddha, it seems, did not find that deep place: he *only* knew desire confused by fear. Thus, the only solution available to him was to eliminate desire.

Our lifelong task is to cooperate with God's gracious action of liberating from fear our desire for fulfillment. That is why, at every crisis of spiritual growth, we hear again the voice of fear: "Where will *I* be? What will become of me?" The art of spiritual discernment is to get to know that voice and to meet it with the question, what do I lack when I am free?

The contrast between the Buddhist and the Christian diagnosis of the human ill is essentially the same as the contrast between the sub-Christian and the Christian understanding of the cross. In the sub-Christian understanding, life is the crucifier, the ego the crucified. In the same way, for the Buddhist analysis, life is the crucifier, desire is the crucifier, the ego the victim. The Buddhist remedy is to eliminate desire, the crucifier. The Christian remedy is to realize that desire is not the crucifier but the crucified—by the ego with its characteristic climate of fear. Our human *eros* is manhandled in a thousand ways, misdirected, distorted, disguised, and eventually rendered hateful to us, by the fear that dogs it. God's sublime remedy for this ill is the symbol of the true self and *eros* of the human as victim, calling us not to the extinction of desire but to sorrow and a second birth.

I have learned this by experience, which is the only school. I can be crucified by a close relationship—driven out of my wits. But the moment of resolution and of light and freedom comes when I perceive that the inflicting element is not the love but *my expectations* of the person: my expectations, which are powered by a horror of the void, and set the person up as the filling of my emptiness. Of this ego-feeling, the love is the victim, not vice versa. The pain involved in accepting and following this insight can be intense, but it is a pain that is incredibly different from what we normally experience as the pain of desire.

3

A PARABLE OF FORGIVENESS

Let us look at the parable of the servant, who, having been forgiven an enormous debt by his master, refused to remit a much smaller debt of his fellow servant.

The truth this parable is getting at in its deceptively simple fairy-tale way is the existential truth that lies at the heart of the human condition: that my hardness of heart in respect of my brother *disguises from me* the fact that I am enormously in God's debt. Instead of saying, "*Although* I have been let off a huge debt, I won't even let someone else off a small one," I should say, "*Because* I see no reason to remit my brother's debt, the forgiveness of God has no serious meaning for me."

This turns the whole thing upside down. Far from my refusal to remit being manifestly outrageous to me in the light of God's forgiveness of me, it is my refusal that is preventing the light from getting through.

At the fairy-tale level, the refusal of the servant incurs severe punishment from the master. But at the existential level, the punishment incurred by our hardness of heart is the punishment *of not seeing* that we are in God's debt and in need of his forgiveness.

The parable taken simply as it stands is a description of the way it *objectively* is between us and God and between us and our fellow humans. It is not, *as it stands*, a description of our *consciousness* or unconsciousness of these relationships. This is our concern. This we must explore if the gospel is to live for us. We must think of God's forgiveness as a transformation of consciousness.

We then realize that the connection between God's forgiveness of us and our forgiveness of each other is *organic*. There is only one experience: of the heart liberated *from* sin *for* our fellow humans. Conversely, the condition of not appreciating myself as in need of the forgiveness of God is the condition of automatically subjecting other people to myself in my thinking. The "normality" of insisting on payment *is* the sense of myself as autonomous, and this is an estimate of myself in which the forgiveness of God has no place.

The more we concentrate on the question, "How, basically, do I see myself?" the clearer this organic oneness of forgiveness needed, and forgiveness given to another becomes. If I know only one center to my life—the ego with its multiple concerns—then I am at a center that does not know the need to be forgiven and that finds it normal to exact payment in one form or another. Conversely, if the mysterious, innerly spatial, *other* center is becoming reality for me, then my ego begins to be "placed" in a spiritual universe that declares its need for God's pardon and the preposterousness of exacting payment from others.

It is in the pardon of God, becoming a need and a reality for me, that other people leap, in my mind, out of the enslaving categories, of enemy or of expected-from friend, into a new and spacious mental world. Does it need to be said that they will notice the difference, or that if they don't, I have been playing games with myself?

It is increasingly a fact of my experience that the deepest, most obscure, and most unavowed obstacle to a total surrender to God's forgiveness lies in the way I look at other people, lies in the system, built up over the years, of expectations and evaluations and projections. Of this fact, the gospel is the one faithful and unflinching reminder. That is why it is indivisibly the witness to the awful majesty of God and to the brother in need. Anyone who reduces either of these dimensions of the gospel to the other is still estranged from his true center where alone Jesus speaks.

This would be clearer if we understood better the relationship between attitude and action. It is simplistic to regard our basic attitude as the "profound" thing, and action as merely symptomatic. As deeply as we *experience* ourselves, we *enact* ourselves. Our ill lies as deeply in the human world we *make* as it lies in the seeds of our motivation. Consequently, the gospel places the remedy of our ill in the acted-out condition of man, the crucifier of life.

There is another place where Jesus uses the down-to-earth image of debt and payment. In the incident of the sinful woman at Simon the Pharisee's house, he tells the story of the two debtors, and concludes "her sins, which were many, have been forgiven; hence she has shown great love" (Luke 7:47). It is not that the woman, being a prostitute, had incurred a larger debt in respect of God than had the punctilious Pharisee. Rather, the extent to which she has entered into the divine realm of forgiveness is *symbolized* by saying, "She has been let off a bigger debt." The extravagant behavior of the lover, contrasted with the correct behavior of the normal pious person, has the privilege of opening up the *true* dimension of the human person, in which one owes millions to a God who happily cancels the debt. The person in whose self-estimate "little has been forgiven" is a person who has seen little of oneself.

It is significant that it is this incident that produces the teasing and paradoxical saying, "Much has been forgiven her because she has loved much." The reason is that here the relationship between divine forgiveness and human behavior has "come off," whereas in the story of the servant it does not come off. It is where the forgiveness of God becomes human fact that we are plunged into paradoxical language and invited to correlate the bizarre behavior of an immoral woman at a dinner party with the remission of an enormous debt on God's bank.

4

GOD AND FORGIVENESS, PART 1

The idea of the divine forgiveness of sin is the most spiritually ambitious of religious ideas, and therefore imposes the greatest labor on the person who would make it one's own. It conjoins the two extremes of human experience: the infinite, all-transcending whole, and a person's most particular experience of one's own life as sordid, trivial, and self-seeking. It conjoins the ultimately sublime with what Becker refers to as "everything painful and sobering in what psychoanalytic genius and religious genius have discovered about man revolves around the terror of admitting what one is doing to earn his self-esteem" (*The Denial of Death*, 6).

Today, many people experience no difficulty in finding meaning in, and desiring for themselves, God's forgiveness of sin. Generally, however, these people evince no sense of the *oddness* of this idea, of the disparateness of the experiences that it bridges. The God whose forgiveness they seek is a God whom traditional religion has for long *associated* with the mental world in which sins are committed. In Freudian terms, this God is the superego minus the latter's merciless rigidity. It is altogether a different matter to connect one's personal sense of meanness, the small mental world of which sin is precisely the *creating*, with the idea of a center of reality indifferent to what we are immemorially habituated to regard as important: the Narcissistic self, the "real" center of custom, of society, of philosophy, of art, of science. To think of *such* a reality as "forgiving sin" is mind-taxing to the limit, possibly, of mind-destruction.

Now, *this* forgiveness is going to work not on "my sins" but on the way in which I *consider myself* as sinful. This *natural* sense of sin is the revulsion at myself that arises in a context in which I am the center of attention. Not revulsion *at* regarding myself as the center, but rather the revulsion-component, the emotionally negative component, *of* the sense of myself as the center. *This sense* is not questioned by the natural sense of sin, which arises *within* it, as its negative component, as the self-disgust that is the negative mood of an inflated self-awareness. This self-disgust stands to an integral sense of sin as a hangover stands to a real growth out of alcoholism. The divine forgiveness is a gracious dissolution of that *system* of self-awareness in which I show up alternately as euphoric and depressed. It touches not the self-important sinner but the sin of self-importance.

In touching *this* sin, the divine forgiveness is *not* acting out of character with its infinite and beyond-me root. On the contrary, self-importance is *properly* dissolved by that infinite and luminous center that is its ultimate corrective. What is meant by the divine forgiveness of sin is that God begins to be God in the small, mean life of the sinner.

This touch of grace, for all that it is in character with its transcendent origin, enters most intimately into the small world of the sinner. It is dissolving that world. It is not ignoring it, or sweeping it aside, or urging me to forget about myself in my Narcissistic wriggle. It is getting into the wriggle, liberating the latter's captive. It is teaching me to experience myself in all the sordid particulars of my life of sin, but with a strange difference. I am being taught to experience all my meanness in a new context. In this learning, I become more not less aware of the meanness. I am invited to contemplate "what I am doing to secure my self-esteem." The divine forgiveness of sin is the gracious presence of a new context for my meanness to experience itself. Its roots are at the luminous unseen heart of the galaxies; its presence is in my sordid particulars.

As this discovery proceeds, I begin to see my meanness as a *making*-mean what is, in itself, not mean. Let me illustrate this. A friend seeks my advice on a recent interchange with a person, in which he obscurely feels he has been obtuse. I point out where I think he might have overlooked something. Immediately he says, "Oh, I'm always doing that. You're so right." No good has come of the dialogue thus far. He has merely swung from the "euphoric" position, in which he has done the damage, to the "depressed" position, in which he "always behaves that way." Incredibly, this swing to a blanket self-denigration is an almost unconscious ruse on his part to *avoid* the truth I want him to examine.

In a moment of light, I might be able to make him see that what is at the root of a troubled relationship with others is something he is doing to himself, is a real potential that he is destroying. The thing we most need to be told, and most resist being told, concerning an experience when we know we have been at fault, is how good we basically and potentially are. Nothing hurts so much as having one's own individual, unique life touched, with its freedom, its responsibility, its unknowing.

Thus, to come into the transcendent forgiveness situation is to reexperience my meanness in a new context that breaks it down into "something I am doing to myself." "Myself, alternately experienced as pleasing and revolting" gives way to "something I am doing to myself." This internal action, in its turn, gives way to the beginning of a dialogue. "Something I am *doing* to myself" turns into a dialogue that I am *having* with myself.

Now it is with the coming of this interior dialogue that the forgiveness situation begins. For now, there is awakening within me, as the victim of my meanness, as the bearer of my own life, the spark of true being that belongs in the totality of being. That which awakens, in a new sorrow and beyond praise and blame, is *my life*, my freedom to be, my responsibility to existence. I begin to think of myself, in my meanness, as touched by the God who is the life center of all being. Far from forgiveness being something the believer seeks from a God already defined by his religion-culture as the forgiver of sin, the very *idea* of forgiveness is experienced as the bridge between the human meanness, normally interpreted in an ego-centered way, and the transcendent center.

The self that I am repressing, immobilizing, alternately enjoying and blaming is the self that demands, in its brittle fragility, the worship of other people. In the critical instance of a grave offense from one of the worshippers, this self assumes its extreme posture of self-securing—the unforgiving posture. In other words, having analyzed the self-immobilizing, self-securing position, we must look at this as it relates to other people. There, we find a continuum, of which the unforgiving situation is only the extremity. *Along* this continuum, we encounter the more normal situation in which the captive self imprisons others in the categories of "objects of our expectation." Even before they are judged unforgivable, they are extensions of my system of self-esteem. This system, which totally breaks down when I receive the grace to forgive an enemy, is already trembling in the balance when I understand that my expectations of others are stemming from what I am doing to myself.

Now we are at the point at which the opening of a person to God's forgiveness, and the yielding of that person's basic stance in respect of others, may be experienced and understood as one same breaking down of the normal system of self-esteem and self-denigration. To forgive an enemy is to risk my entire system. To open myself to the forgiveness of God is to risk my entire system. It is the same risk. Jesus' insistence on the forgiveness of enemies, as though that were the whole substance of salvation, is based on a perception of this identity in the risk. He is saying, "Take the risk there"—where the presence of another human being, selfish and mean like yourself, precludes any possibility of bullshit. In that sense, to forgive one's enemy *is* the whole of salvation. If *that* is happening in a person's life, the forgiveness of God is happening in its primary meaning.

We can therefore paraphrase "Forgive us our offenses as we forgive those who have offended us" thus: "Grant us to experience that true divine forgiveness whose working in us is the dissolution of our normal unforgiving system." "Forgive us our sins, *in the way of* us forgiving each other." "Forgive us our sins *as* 'us forgiving each other'—that is to say, truly." It must have struck many people that there is something odd about this petition. We couldn't be asking God to model and measure his forgiveness of us by the forgiveness we manage to accord, sometimes through clenched teeth, to each other. Yet the forgiveness of man by man *is*, in the wording of the prayer, the model. "As we forgive." The only resolution of this problem is to say that God's forgiveness is pictured in *that* inter-human forgiveness that is its mirror image, a mirror image that only appears in human experience when the central light has come on, when God has made himself known to us in the forgiveness of sin. "Forgive us our sins so we can see it, live it, in a new community."

The gospel has received two different descriptions. One is this: "The gospel is the proclamation of God's gratuitous forgiveness, a forgiveness apprehended in faith and expressed in sacrament." The other: "The gospel is the one really radical ethic, based on the forgiveness of our enemies." There is no disjunction here. The first is the transcendental analytic description; the second is the existential. Both are contained in the statement that the gospel is the one definitive statement on the forgiveness of sin. The gospel is doing two complementary things. It is presenting a *real* idea of God's forgiveness, as opposed to the idea that we form in the attempt to placate a God of our making. It is presenting a *real* idea of our forgiveness by another, as opposed to the forgiveness we sometimes just find place for in our immemorial and acculturated egoism. The normal idea of God's forgiveness and the normal idea of human forgiveness belong to and express one system of human self-estimation with the ego at the center, having God as its chaplain and the suitably repentant enemy as its beneficiary. Correspondingly, the real idea of God's forgiveness and the real idea of human forgiveness belong to and express the system of the new person in critical and penitent and growing dialogue with oneself.

Finally, the divine forgiveness that works itself out at the heart of our meanness has for its all-powerful and all-gathering symbol the Man on the cross. For that symbol tells us that sin is the destruction of the good that is in us. It takes us beyond the cop-out whereby we compensate a euphoric self-esteem with self-denigration, into the dialogue between the crucifier and the crucified that is at the heart of every person. In the final analysis, the sorrow that is the place of all forgiveness is not even the sorrow of the crucifier but the sorrow of the crucified. The wellspring of conversion, perhaps only discerned later when the conversion situation has matured, is that which belongs to the true God-implanted self as we awake on the cross where sin has placed us. The heart of Christian sorrow is the Man of Sorrows.

5

GOD AND FORGIVENESS, PART 2

When one person forgives another, the change happens in the forgiving person. We say that he "relents," abandons his uptight stance. Yet when God forgives, it is the forgiven person's heart that is changed. Human forgiveness is the unhardening of the heart of the pardoner; divine forgiveness is the unhardening of the heart of the pardoned.

This contrast is the basis of the connection between being forgiven by God and "forgiving one's brother from the heart." For in the case of God's forgiveness, the *essence* of being forgiven is the unhardening of the heart, which is the *essence* of our forgiveness by another. That which *originates* human forgiveness, the unhardening of the heart, is *originated* by divine forgiveness.

If we ignore this difference between divine and human forgiving, we are confined to saying, "You have been forgiven (by God); therefore, you *in your turn* should forgive your brother."

But if we confine ourselves to this human model, we must consider that though the relenting takes place in the pardoner, he who receives pardon only truly does so by allowing his heart to be changed. The real fault of the servant in the parable consists not in refusing forgiveness to his fellow servant, but

113

in not appreciating the forgiveness he has received. To be forgiven is to be set free, which should raise the question, free to do what? Certainly not to continue one's tyranny over others.

While the forgiveness of a man can be received without appreciation—as the immense relief of being able to cancel that ugly figure in one's balance sheet—the divine forgiveness cannot be received *at all* without appreciation. Appreciation is its substance. The changing of the heart is its substance, and of that substance we must give or eliminate it from our experience. The divine forgiveness either creates a community or it is not received.

6

PERSONAL EXPERIENCE AND PAUL

The following experience led to the formulation of the principle of inversion, which is central to our theme. I was giving a course of lectures, which, so far as I could judge, were going very well. One day, a close friend asked me, "How was this morning's class?" "Good," I replied, "they're really the best lot I've had." He replied that he had overheard a few members of the class saying they hadn't a clue where I was going and were very frustrated. I went to my room and sat like a stone. Although I had a talk to give in an hour, I could not turn my mind to it. I was dead, destroyed, and angry.

After about half an hour, I thought vaguely of the cross and the new thoughts I was beginning to have about it. In connection with the painful experience I had just had, I began to ask, "What's going on here?" *Somehow* the suggestion then formed itself (and not in answer to the question, "Who's crucifying whom?" which only came into my system *because of* this experience) that, contrary to my *feeling* of being crucified by my friend's information, it was my ego, with its inveterate euphoria, that was the crucifier, the class—or rather the true situation between the class and myself—the crucified. Euphoria is a great destroyer of life with its vast variety of tones and shades. It will have everything to be going splendidly—or else it will resign. Meanwhile life is trying to breathe. This student has understood. That one has not. That other one thinks he has but has understood something else, and so on. But the ego will have none of this, and its first target—though not easily spotted—is my self, my body, the actual communications that are going out to those men and women.

With this thought, I began to revive, with a new feeling for my class, for myself, and for life. In an hour, I knew that I had made a very important discovery.

I see now what Paul means by crucifying the flesh. The flesh is the ego. Yet I have argued that the ego is never crucified, only *thinks* of itself as crucified until I discover the true cross in a situation. Despite appearances and immediate reaction, the ego is crucifier, but *then* I must identify with the crucified part, with the truth, with my true self. *This* move is death to the ego, and *then* life to me who is thus freed from the ego's tyranny.

To crucify the ego is not to act against it. To crucify the ego's lusts is not to repress them. It is to put the ego on that cross *that itself is inflicting*, and thus to undergo death in the ego, or death as far as the ego is concerned, and so to find life in the crucified self.

The Pauline askesis of crucifying the ego-flesh, once it is grasped, opens the door to the following Pauline description of the new condition of humankind in Christ Jesus. "So if anyone is in Christ, there is a new creation: everything old has passed away; see, everything has become new!" (2 Cor 5:17). The newness consists in the fact that a person who finds oneself in Christ goes through a door on the other side of which everything is reversed. The basis of this reversal is the reversal of the ego's version of crucified and crucifier; the follow-through is the self-identification with the crucified in the situation, which means death to the ego and a new flourishing of the person's real being. This death to the ego, death to the ego in this Spirit-directed and wholly creative process, is "mortification." We do not hear this word anymore. In the period immediately preceding its demise, it had come to mean a dreary sort of emotional hari-kari, and as such was then rejected on this time-honored principle: first play the tune wrong, then stop playing it altogether. In the meantime, breezy, well-intentioned spirits say that all Paul is talking about is self-discipline, so let's call it that instead of "mortification." This is not what Paul is talking about. He is talking about the mystery of the crucified as it daily enlarges our lives in freeing us from our ego-illusions. Far from being an emotional hari-kari, mortification is an emotional liberation, turning the energy that we expend in unconsciously strangling our life into freeing it.

We can then understand the texts in which Paul describes the new life as freed from sin. The fact that this freeing process must be gone through again and again as our ever-changing life meets new challenges does not alter the fact that structurally, and each time it happens, the liberation is definitive, an end and a beginning. The Christian life is not a continual struggle against sin in which sin *gradually* yields to grace. It is the process of repeated appropriation, in ever new circumstances, of a *total* and definitive ending of sin and beginning of life. The process viewed over a time span is of course gradual. But in its interior, it is rather a series of quantum leaps, each leap being constituted by a death of the ego-flesh. The heart of the process is the each-time total death and unpowering of the ego, rendered possible by the self-manifestation of the crucified as the structure of the believing heart; by the presence, that is, of the self as the crucified, in whose favor the ego is called on to surrender.

It is fatally easy to impose on Paul's exposition the principles of a commonsense askesis of struggle against bad habits. Surely these are what Paul means by sin. And, of course, the converted have resolved to struggle against it. They decree an end to sin simply as a person does when he makes a good resolution. Obviously, that's what Paul is talking about! But it's not what Paul says. This commonsense understanding ignores Paul's statement, "You also must consider yourselves dead to sin and alive to God in Christ Jesus" (see Rom 6). Paul's charge against his Corinthian converts was not that they weren't keeping up the struggle against bad habits, but that they weren't letting Christ work in them, that they didn't realize what had happened to them, what they had in them, what they had it in them to become. Nor do we.

Liberation from sin is rooted in the *forgiveness* of sin only when sin is understood as the tyranny of self-worship, revealed in Christ as at root self-crucifixion, and resolved in the faithful vision of the crucified. In this ultimate form of forgiveness, in which *God* forgives, it is in the forgiven person, not in the pardoner, that "relenting" happens. Thus, the freedom that, in an interpersonal situation, is generally experienced more by the forgiver than the forgiven, in the divine forgiveness is wholly in the forgiven. We are let off from worshipping ourselves. God lets us off from worshipping ourselves, and so frees us for life.

Thus, we have two choices for our understanding of Paul: a holistic interpretation and a commonsense interpretation. In the commonsense interpretation, sin has its common meaning. God has forgiven our sins—by some wonderful arrangement God has made with Christ. Yet sin still stays with us—"the one that got away," or our bad habits—for us to struggle with. There's no connection between God's forgiveness and this continued affair with sin. God's forgiveness does not mean the end of sin *in us*, except as perhaps inspiring a good resolution. In the holistic interpretation, God in Christ has revealed the root of sin in us as self-crucifixion, and so enabled us to experience his forgiveness as the liberation of us from ourselves, a liberation that we enjoy anew each time we find the cross in our lives, identify with the crucified, and so let the ego die. In this view, forgiveness equals liberation, and liberation powers the ongoing askesis. Thus, the Christian life is simply the prolongation of God's forgiveness of humankind in Christ.

Appendix

CHRISTIAN
SELF-DISCOVERY[1]

The thought of Bernard Lonergan centers on the most important fact about the human subject. Among the continually expanding number of facts about this most complex and intriguing being, the most important is that he is self-transcending. All the writing of Lonergan is, in one way or another, heading the reader towards the recognition of this fact *about himself*. Self-transcendence is personally discovered to be the case, or it is not properly understood. And into this discovery one is dragged, protesting, kicking and screaming. For on the journey inward towards this recognition—for which the Augustinian word confession is the most appropriate— one travels through all sorts of subsidiary systems of oneself, each deploying its own characteristic distracting virtuosity and complaining against a threatened takeover. The struggle is similar to the Ignatian journey towards a devastatingly honest and grace-enabled self-appraisal, which also is a journey through protests—styles of living, slowly assembled and established to meet life's challenges as best one could, protest that life on any terms other than theirs is simply impossible. At the end of both journeys—or better, of both modalities of the

---

1. This paper was originally read at the Lonergan Workshop, Boston College, USA, 1976.

one journey—the self that is revealed as *my* self, and that can no more be doubted than I can doubt that I exist, is a lover, is generous, finds peace in the other, lives in a limitless universe, is self-transcending.

Self-transcendence, then, is not a property to be attributed to a being called "man." It is something to be discovered about myself. It is something that *is* discovered insofar as I discover myself. The discovery of the self carries the discovery of self-transcendence within it. The correct assertion "man is self-transcending" invites us first to conceive, somehow, of a being called man, and *then* to *add*, as a notion distinct from the notion of this being, that it is self-transcending. But the discovery I am speaking of works differently. In it, the notion of self-transcendence is not *added*, but grows out of the self as freshly appropriated and acknowledged—grows out of as the only way I can henceforth understand or speak about myself. What is absolutely essential to the discovery is that the intimacy, the "I-ness," of the self, has self-transcendence as its structure; that the realization "that is I," with all its undeniable sense of homecoming and a huge familiarity, invokes love as its meaning. "I am" equals "I love." "I love" is the only way to say "I am."

But this discovery is not made by "going into oneself." St. Teresa writes sometimes about "going into oneself," but this phrase is, for her, only a sometimes-appropriate shorthand for what she does in contemplative prayer. It is only the self as realized in some great and mysterious adventure that reveals, as its deepest secret, that it is lover. The obstacles to true self-discovery are many, formidable, tortuous, and perverse. They are only cleared through some unaccountable generosity that can occur in the very thick of our total involvement with others and with the God who queers our pitch with others and with ourselves until we accept the grace to let him speak. In what follows, I want to examine the most intense and crucial of all our involvements: the situation of offense, of hurt, of forgiveness, of reconciliation, and, finally, of that human guilt which, beyond the reach of even the most loving and patient of friends, eats away the self and challenges an infinite love to dissolve it. It is in a true and accurate assessment of this situation, above all, that we may hope to discern that the human subject is indeed lover. The battle-scarred being who in this most human of all situations eventually opens his eyes and smiles, is a self-entangled lover. The skilled love that seeks him out seeks *that* in him; for that is who he is. A forgiveness that does not believe *that* of him is no forgiveness and will only compound the misery.

I have been led to this theme by a classroom experience of the last semester. Teaching theology to freshmen and sophomores who only come to me in the fetters of "the theology requirement," I found that an extensive and sophisticated analysis of the structure of forgiveness between people awoke much interest and solicited some remarkable end-of-term papers. From this I came to two conclusions: that forgiveness, and all that it involves and all that involves it, are the things that interest God most, and that the things that interest God most are the things people are most interested in. The first conclusion comes as the end of a persistent meandering study of the gospel that has to be measured in decades. The second, though crashingly obvious, has taken and is taking courage to implement.

My treatment falls into five sections:

1. A human forgiveness situation. Its implication is that the hurt we deliver is at root our self-hatred, the suppression of the lover in us. So forgiveness is only *received* through, or in, or as fostering, self-acceptance.
2. Having considered the *interpersonal* situation of forgiveness, I zero in on the *forgiven subject*. How

does *he* stand in relation to his fault? I find that, integral to his reception of forgiveness, integral to his revival as lover, is a very accurate, free, and full admission of his fault. And for this to be possible, he must have an extraordinary confidence in being accepted. Jesus understands this structure, operative between people, as the very structure of the soul and involved in its ultimate healing. So the theme of this section is Jesus' treatment of sinners as described in the gospel.

3. I find that, grounding and profoundly enriching the gospel concept of sinfulness is the concept, wrestled with by Paul, of enmity with God. So, correspondingly, grounding and profoundly enriching the gospel concept of forgiveness is the Pauline concept of reconciliation. This is the full meaning of our acceptance: the release from enmity, the release of the lover.

4. I ask the deepest question: What is it in us that radically inhibits belief that we are accepted? This brings us to a guilt that precedes and exceeds the moral sphere. The theme of this section is the full and final confrontation between Jesus and the sinner: the cross and the resurrection.

5. Finally, I discern a need to correlate this *generic guilt* from which the gospel exonerates us, with the *sins* of which we are justly ashamed.

THE STRUCTURE OF FORGIVENESS

What happens when Mary, who loves John, forgives him for an injury he has done her? What is involved, in her and in him, in this transaction?

On her side, she continues to love him, and to let him know it, not primarily in words but in the wordless way that is open to lovers.

On his side, he "hears" from her that she still loves him, so he "hears" from her that he is still lovable, still of value. But at the same time, he is experiencing himself *not* as of value, but as having treated someone badly.

Thus, her love is setting up a contradiction, in him, between "I am good" and "I am bad."

The only resolution of this contradiction is for him to see that in hurting her he is hurting himself. This resolves the contradiction, for it makes John's badness consist in attacking, striking at, his own goodness. I can be, at one and the same time, good and bad, *if* my badness consists in the suppression of my goodness.

Now this is precisely what her love is telling him: that what he takes to be badness in himself is the suppression of his goodness. It is *not* that he is "no good."

This brings us to the most important thing about true forgiveness; namely, it is the opposite of what we normally think forgiveness is. The normal understanding of "being forgiven" is "I am bad, *but* you forgive me." I *am* no good, but *even so*, you're *so* good that you forgive me. Whereas true forgiveness means Mary reawakening John's sense of *his own* goodness, which has taken a big knock from the way he's treated Mary. True forgiveness is love in action awakening the offender to the good he suppressed *in himself* in hitting out at the offended one.

The point is that when I have hurt someone, the easy and natural way for me to level with that fact is to regard myself as a lousy, no-good person. My pride prefers to keep it that way. That is why it so often happens, when someone has hurt another, that he *keeps repeating*, "I'm just a selfish bastard, what else can you expect?" This *sounds* as though he's admitting his fault, being very humble, taking the blame, but *really* he's using these words *in order to* stop her forgiving love from getting to him. He doesn't want to hear that he is good in this situation that he can only level with by thinking of himself as bad. He prefers not to face the *full* situation, which is that he has hurt another person *by shrinking himself.* When you hurt another person, your true self, the lover in you, goes into hiding, and uses every possible ruse to stay in hiding. Even abject apology!

So the full experience of being forgiven *is*, *first of all*, the experience of a sharp contrast between "being an offender" (being offensive) and "failing myself," and *then* the invitation to *move* from the first self-description (as offensive) to the second (as failing myself). Above all, the experience is a poignant sense of the love (Mary's) that is enabling one to make this rather amazing move. For Mary's love is essential here. If John, without considering her at all, says, "All that's happened is that I failed to live up to my full potential," he is an impossibly smug person.

In sum, true forgiveness does not merely "forgive the offender." It awakens him to his true being that he rejected in being an offender. It restores to the offender the dignity of being a self-forgetful lover. Forgiveness is a restoration to the self, and is the climate in which the *meaning* of the self has its clearest radiance.

THE FORGIVEN SUBJECT

When we concentrate on the forgiven subject, we encounter a paradox. While it is an obsession with how bad he had been that inhibits his reception of forgiveness, it is also the case that a person can only fully confess to his fault when he is certain of receiving it. I cannot admit that I have done wrong; I cannot admit that I have made a huge mistake, except to someone who I know accepts me. The person who cannot admit that he is wrong is desperately insecure. At root, he does not feel accepted, and so he represses his guilt, he covers his tracks, and so we get the paradox: confession of fault means a good self-concept. Repression of fault means a bad self-concept.

Jesus understood, as no one else has at such depth and with such simplicity, that this simple fact *between* people manifests something in the very structure of the soul. He knew that a person's deepest insecurity is caused by a sense of guilt accompanied with no sense of being accepted. He found a way to open people's eyes to themselves as accepted by God, so that they could, in the serene confidence of this acceptance, confess their sins. He went further, in that he brought people to an act of confession that was *itself* the supreme act of confidence in God's acceptance. In this way, he brought about the greatest spiritual revolution that ever occurred. Religious man had done *everything* with guilt except totally acknowledge it. Jesus enabled man to do just this. He made this possible by enabling him to feel accepted in his very being. At a hitherto unknown level of acceptance and confession, he lifted definitively the burden of guilt that, at every other level, man can only shift around. He actualized, between man and his Maker, the structure of admission-in-acceptance that we discover between ourselves. We have yet to bring this structure down to its deepest level of operation. This must wait until we consider "generic guilt."

This is the logic of the gospel concept of sin and forgiveness. The consciousness of sin that Jesus awakens in people is something completely new in the history of religion. The newness consists in being enabled to say "I have sinned" in the way a man can sometimes say "I am sorry" to his wife or his friend, namely, in a way that gives expression to his utter certainty of being accepted. The gospel confession of sin is the most generous, secure, adventurous expression of the human heart. It is the risk that is only taken in the certainty of being acceptable and accepted. It is the full and final expression of that confidence. Only to your lover do you expose your worst. To an amazed world, Jesus presents a God who calls for this confession only so that he may reveal himself in a person's depths as his lover. This confession, in a context of divine acceptance, releases the deepest energies of the human spirit, and constitutes the gospel revolution in its essence.

The most important characters in the gospel drama are those "publicans and sinners" we have heard about since our Christian childhood. They are important because they most clearly illustrate *that* consciousness of sin which cripples the spirit. They are the people whom society has told they are bad. Their sense of guilt has eaten into their very identity, therefore, and made them unacceptable to themselves or to anybody else. Jesus awakens in them a sense of acceptance, so that they can acknowledge their sin in the certainty of being accepted. He does not say, "Society says you are doing wrong but I say you are not." Prostitution and the rip-off of the tax collectors is a destructive way of life, and Jesus knows this. What he says is "you can acknowledge your wrongdoing in a way that exposes you to the acceptance of God."

"You have heard that it was said, 'You shall not commit adultery.' But I say to you that everyone who looks at a woman with lust has already committed adultery with her in his heart" (Matt 5:27–28). The intention behind this statement is to bring good people who would stop short of adultery to recognize the sin that is in us all and that now at last can find confession and acceptance. It is to promote good people to the status of sinners, who can *then* be promoted to the status of unfaithful lovers. Robert Frost has expressed this well in *A Masque of Mercy*:

Christ came to introduce a break with logic
That made all other outrage seem as child's play:
The Mercy on the Sin against the Sermon.
Strange no one ever thought of it before Him.
'Twas lovely and its origin was love.

He goes on to explain that curious phrase "The Mercy on the Sin against the Sermon":

Paul's constant theme. The Sermon on the Mount
Is just a frame-up to insure the failure
Of all of us, so all of us will be
Thrown prostrate at the Mercy Seat for Mercy.[2]

This is perhaps the place to remark that the gospel exposure of the roots of sin in the heart is ruinous outside the context of divine acceptance in which alone Jesus makes this exposure. You then get what François Mauriac, in *La Pharisienne*, called the "Furies of the New Covenant."

Let us now return to the basic logic of the gospel of forgiveness. It is, as I have indicated, paradoxical. The paradox may be expressed thus:

Admission of fault   =   a good self-concept

Repression of fault   =   a bad self-concept

Unfortunately, the Christian tradition has screwed up this paradox. By the way in which teachers talk about sin, the "equals" signs have got misplaced thus:

Admission of fault   :   a good self-concept
Repression of fault   :   a bad self-concept

---

2. Robert Frost, *A Masque of Mercy* (New York: Henry Holt & Co., 1975).

Thus, the admission of fault runs "I am a miserable sinner, a no-good bastard." And conversely, the only "good self-concept" that the teachers recognized and correctly upbraided is the smug self-satisfaction obtained by repressing fault. So the "equals" signs go diagonally across the diagram.

The task of rectifying this error is immense. It means learning to read the gospel without hearing its words on the "tapes" of centuries of Christian programming. "God will forgive you, but first you must confess your sin." Isn't that what the gospel says? Yes, but the meaning is "confess your sin so that God can reveal himself to your heart as your lover and friend and so your heart can come alive again, the lover in you can be reborn."

It has taken me thirty years to understand that the admission and forgiveness of sin is the essence of the New Testament. The recovery of this truth is seriously compromised by centuries of misunderstanding. For it is the delicate operation of recovering this truth from the well-meaning people who, repelled by the negative understanding of it, have placed the essence somewhere else. This complex error must be redeemed if we are ever to feel again the magic of Jesus, which promotes "man the sinner" to the dignity of man the unfaithful lover.

ENMITY WITH GOD AND RECONCILIATION

We've already said a good deal about God. We bounced off the John and Mary story freely, and likened God's forgiveness of the sinner to Mary's forgiveness of John. And then, in the second section, we said that the dependence of confession on acceptance works with God as well as with each other. But now we've got to deal fairly and squarely with the fact that

God isn't a bit like Mary or anyone else; for the simple reason that we can't see him or touch him or hear him or experience him in the way that one person experiences another. We may say, as Jesus does in effect say, that God's attitude to us is one of acceptance, as Mary's is in our story, but how do we *experience* God as behaving toward us in this way?

There's a real problem here, and for God's sake let's recognize it, otherwise we shall never appreciate the deep mystical dimension of God's love. The problem shows up once we recognize the crucial difference between *saying* that God behaves like the Father of the Prodigal Son, and *mediating*, making available, this behavior of God. The bright kid in the religion lesson appreciates that the appearing of God at the level of *meanings* does not tell us whether God *is* or is a Father. He's onto the same thing. The *likening* of God to the forgiving person whom John experiences in Mary is not the *making available* of God to our experience as one who loves and liberates.

I have said that God is quite unlike Mary in that he is not visible or tangible or audible or kissable. Now this *cause* of unlikeness, this *ratio* of his unlikeness, is per se a theme for *mistrust* rather than trust. Heavily prejudiced already in the direction of non-self-acceptance, we are to that extent in need of visible and tangible support, and this is precisely what we don't get from an invisible, intangible God. So his absence makes him suspect at the soul's gut-level where assurance is so desperately sought and where even the goodness of friends is often unavailing.

This basic existential mistrust of God underlies all historical religion, though it is not avowed. Let's look at historical religion for a moment. By religion, I mean simply the *existential* negotiation of God as opposed to the purely *cognitive*. Now I suppose that there are two ingredients in man's religious negotiation of God. One is, of course, man's self-transcendence, the yearning of his spirit for the All. But there is another ingredient which really contradicts the first, and actively inhibits its flowering, in other words, inhibits recognition of God as the all-originating love-energy by man the lover. This other ingredient is constituted not by *wonder* at our being but by an acute *unhappiness* with it, a sense of worthlessness, of insignificance. With this "wretched" creature man, with this self-fulfilling prophecy of failure, God is *contrasted*. This is one of the great Old Testament themes: the power, the splendor, the holiness, the sublimity of God, as against this worm that is man.

Now there *is* of course a contrast between the infinite and the finite, but *motivating* the contrast is a sense of worthlessness. The God who is so great is the God who regards *us* as nothing. At the limit, God becomes the very name for our worthlessness, the Ultimate Reality whose nonacceptance of us confirms our suspicion that we are not acceptable. Thus pushed to the limit, the God-of-the-sense-of-worthlessness is the exact opposite to the God-of-the-sense-of-self-transcendence and, if allowed to, would blot him out.

It never comes to that of course. Though note the savage cruelty and self-destructiveness of much pagan religious practice. And, for that matter, look at the God of Jung's *Answer to Job*.

Now the God Jesus is talking about is a God who is experienced *only* through the sense of self-transcendence and *not at all* through the sense of worthlessness. And this is a God *never heard of before*, for the simple reason that never before Jesus was there a *man* totally without the sense of worthlessness.

We are going to see later how Jesus gets this nearly impossible message through to us. Suffice it to say here that once the message *had* got through, Paul could cry out "My God, don't think, you people, that we *loved* God! We hated him! Tell it like it is. Now that we are reborn we see in retrospect with what resentment our sense of worthlessness took it out on God, though of course, we always kept religious good manners. Now at last we are *reconciled* to him. Yes, reconciliation is of *us* to *God*, not of God to us."

The end of the story is that man the lover is completely vindicated, justified, acquitted, and that's what the love of God is. This is the resurrection, the hatching of man the lover out of the thick millennial cocoon of man the sinner. How, at the climax of the story, Jesus becomes man the sinner, will be the theme of the next section.

GENERIC GUILT

Do I dare
Disturb the universe?

—T. S. Eliot, "The Love Song of J. Alfred Prufrock"

Now at last I've got to think about guilt. I need to get a *generic* notion of guilt, some idea of its general shape before it enters into all the distinctions such as that between neurotic guilt and reasonably acknowledged guilt. What is guilt, most generally conceived? What, generically, occasions it?

It is very closely associated with freedom. The girl who decides to leave home feels guilt, mainly perhaps because of her mother. The child who plays with another child of whom his parents do not approve, or who even *thinks* otherwise than his parents about this matter of friends, feels guilty. And the great myth of the fall, that dominates the Christian tradition, presents guilt as arising, as it were automatically and in the nature of things, when the man and the woman make a bid for independent judgment, for making the world their world, its good and evil their good and evil.

In other words, guilt seems to be the accusation of some enclosing whole or order against one who breaks out from it. "How could you do this to us?" asks the family, or the religious order, or—more radically—the psychic womb. The all-pervading, all-beautifying world of "participation mystique" cries out in gentle outrage and pain against the newly self-aware and self-disposing. How could you do this to us? Now you are alone. How will you be without our comfort? Now you are forlorn, with only yourself to consult. Where will you go? What comfort can you now find within your independent existence, you who but yesterday fed sleepily at the breast of an all-embracing life-power?

Guilt, then, is the accusation that freedom draws from the psychic womb whence it breaks out. It grows with consciousness itself. More accurately, it grows with self-consciousness. That independent self which begins to sally forth in this world carries, from the very start, a baggage of accusations from the blissful world of unconscious childhood. "You're on your own now!"

Thus guilt, in its most radical form, is not generated by the nonconformity of my action with the relevant social mores. It inheres in my action precisely as a free, as opposed to a "being-part-of," action. Its gravamen is not nonconformity but independence. It is hardly distinguishable from loneliness.

Now the next thing to consider is how a person *handles* this inbuilt accusation. He is not, and it seems he cannot be, untouched by it. What I think we do is allow to the accusation its description of what we are doing, and say, "Hell! I'm going ahead in any case." We consent to being *guiltily* on our own, *guiltily* about our own business. We *accept* the psychic womb's description of our independence as "filthy." I believe that the note of *defilement* that Ricoeur finds to be absolutely fundamental to the notion of evil, arises precisely at this point. The contrast between what ridiculous, pretentious, independent little "I" generates and this huge enclosing world of earth and sky is one in which I appear dirty. With my individual mark, I deface the universe. Whence, for instance, came the idea, so easily ridiculed by liberals, that sex was "dirty"? Was it simply the geographical proximity and in part identity between its organs and the organs of excretion? Surely no, the "dirty" bit got in with the "mine alone" bit, and inextricably mixed up with it. A man or a woman, in almost every known culture, hides his or her sex organs not, I suspect, because they are sex organs but because they are *his* or *hers*. They are even *called* "private parts." And it may be that sexuality is, of all areas of human experience and experiment, the most guilt-ridden precisely because here we have the most dramatic conjunction of the universal life force (the psychic womb bit) with the mine and the yours of the self-conscious, self-emancipating individual. Human sexuality is the dramatic breach with the life force, the defacement of the universe by conscious people. It is a use of the impersonal life force that is highly personal, original, adventurous, bizarre, perverse, beautiful.

In summary, guilt is "the human animal persisting in what the psychic womb accuses him of: accepting the latter's description of what he is doing, and doing it none the less." We see then how closely guilt is involved with freedom.

These two elements: the acceptance by our freedom of our earlier world's disapproving description of it, and the persistence in our independence under this description, form, with the accusation itself, the structure of guilt. Accusation, acknowledgment, and persistence. We carry into our new world of freedom the accusations of the old world that bore and nurtured us.

"What are *you* doing?" says the universe to this upstart man. "Why did you do that?" asks the nun of the child. "Because I wanted to." "Do you *always* do what you want to?" Into the very heart of individual conscious action there is injected that note of privacy, of theft, of cornering something off for oneself, which is sounded off by "the whole." And when the family or the religious community accuses the one who leaves it, it is this archetypal structure that is operating. The community's protest and the resultant painful interchange constitute the diachronic dimension. The structure of accusation, acknowledgment, and persistence constitute the synchronic dimension.

"It goes a good deal deeper than what people call their conscience," says Harry in Eliot's play, *The Family Reunion*. "It is just the cancer that eats away the self." The guilt with which the human race has to deal is far more than the memory of heinous deeds. It is the coloration of human self-conscious activity by an indignant cosmos. And whether or not a person does things that can rationally be judged to be bad, his primal sense of guilt precedes and itself colors these doings. Thus, another may forgive him for them, but his forgiveness will come up against the *core* sense of guilt and there founder.

And this last consideration takes us a major step further on our inquiry. If *I*, conscious I, am somehow against the whole; if I am my own doing; if I am stolen from the whole; if I am this private thing of my own inventing; if I am a defilement, a defacing mark; *how can I be acceptable*? How can I be welcomed into the whole whence I have cut myself off, whence I *am* the cutting-off? The problem of the forgiveness of sin is at root the problem of the *acceptance* of the forgiveness of sin, which is what Tillich calls the acceptance of acceptance. It is terribly hard to accept the embrace in a heart that has grown solitary. The difficulty of a middle-aged bachelor in coming into love is one diachronic enactment of the synchronic structure that we have now built up into a fourfold structure: accusation, acknowledgment, persistence, and then nonexpectation of acceptance.

Christian belief places at the climax of its story a man without sin. Does this mean that Jesus was without *guilt*, without that generic guilt of which I have spoken, which seems to be an inalienable part of the coming of individual consciousness?

And if so, what are we to make of the consciousness of Jesus? On my showing at least, human consciousness without guilt is hardly conceivable. At least we may not draw on any examples from our experience or from history or from literature. (And least of all, be it noted, the experience of saints.) But then this mystifying quality, in such a Jesus, of *consciousness without guilt* is balanced or complemented by another quality, equally mystifying, of intimacy with the Absolute, which, most would I think agree, appears to differ qualitatively from the religious experience of all the other great religious leaders. In other words, the absence in Jesus of self-securing against the whole is one side of a coin of which the other is a total certainty of *acceptance* by the whole. And this, it hardly needs saying, not in the manner of the happy preconscious animal. Jesus is not pre-Adamic man. He belongs to the future rather than to the past.

Out of this consciousness Jesus proclaims, and cannot but proclaim, the universal forgiveness of sin. In a consciousness that knows nothing of "acknowledged rejection," he knows a God who accepts. He proclaims this God as one who always forgives. The source and matrix of the Christian conviction of God's forgiving love is the guiltless consciousness of Jesus. Thus "the God and Father of our Lord Jesus Christ" and "the Lover of all" are *conceptually* identical. God's unique presence to Jesus is the ground of his proclamation of God's forgiveness.

But the interaction between people and the phenomenon of a guiltless accepter of acceptance would be complex. For one who is free of guilt altogether, free even of the generic guilt, will be a terrible accusation to me. He will make me conscious of the guilt in my whole buildup as a person. In his presence, my life is undone. Layer by layer, the assemblage in guilty independence is exposed. I am bewildered by the terrible presence of an alternative to what has seemed to me and to everyone else to be the only way to live, the only way to become. And yet the whole *message* of this presence is, that the *accusation* of the psychic womb against my freedom *has no claim on me*, that the self-conscious life which contracted this stigma is, in reality, the most beautiful thing in the cosmos and most acceptable to God and accepted by him. This dismantling of my life effected by the presence of Jesus is only what is produced by the searching fingers of love. But can *I* feel it this way? Can I sense the fingers of love? No, at first it is the threat that I feel.

And so we get a paradox. The *presence* of the guiltless one accuses my guilt, awakens guilt long forgotten and indeed hardly perceived as guilt: while the *message* of the guiltless one is precisely that I am *not* guilty, that the charge against my freedom was falsely pressed and mistakenly accepted.

There is no resolution of this paradox at the level at which it occurs. For guilt, as I have analyzed it, is the very cement of my building. Totally without it, totally deprived of my private self-affirming, I would fall apart, I would die. The only resolution is for him to undergo the death that I would die if I could accept his message of acceptance by God. *He* must die the death of the old world. *He* must fall apart. The love with which he offers man the sinner God's acceptance must turn back on him as death.

And thus, we begin to understand those features of the Pauline soteriology that are the deepest, the hardest, the hardest to understand, and the most easily misunderstood. These are (1) Jesus' death as substitutionary, (2) the strong statement that "God made him to be sin for us," (3) the image of Jesus as embodiment of the old Israel that had to die for God to appear.

We seem to have grasped the crucial point at which our guilt is transferred to Jesus. It is the logic that makes the bearer of the good news its first victim: the victim in whom we find our peace.

It is in the death of Jesus that our perception of him as accusation dissolves into the true perception of him as the sign of our acceptance. For, as we have seen, it is his death that resolves the paradox which held his message of acceptance trapped in the form of accusation.

But it is only in the experience of Jesus as risen that this new perception can come to us. For the risen life of Jesus means this: that the death that is the only way out from the paradox of divine acceptance of man the acceptance-repeller leads into the true life of man as the accepted of God.

It is not just death that is crowned with resurrection. It is the death of the old man. It is the death that God's acceptance seems to involve to the guilty freedom of man, and that is accepted by the proclaimer of this acceptance. It is the violent death that is the second name of the sinless proclaimer of God's acceptance of sinners. For it should not need saying that the synchronic structure that entails the transfer of death-inviting guilt from us to Jesus is worked out diachronically as the violence that comes from the interpretation of love as accusation. We kill "our accuser." In the resurrection, we encounter "our lover."

It begins to be clear to me that the blood of the cross flows, symbolically, from a life assembled with guilt, that guilt which is the oldest ingredient in what we know as self-conscious man. For it is at the *generic* level that the structure of "accusation, acknowledgment, persistence, non-expectation of acceptance" is assembled whose dismantling is the passion and death of the Lord, whose total alternative is the resurrection.

Note

The main contention of this section is that moral guilt is not the adequate category for understanding the gospel of redemption. For this understanding, we need to consider that more radical guilt which virtually equates with loneliness or forlornness and which excludes, or rather repels, divine acceptance. It is something very underattended to. I can only recall a few haunting sentences in Kierkegaard, and some fine observation in Eric Neumann's *The Origins and History of Consciousness*. It also occurs to me that Scheler's "ressentiment," surely the most horrible observation ever achieved by a philosopher, is the reaction of generic guilt to the freedom of another.[3]

GUILT AND SIN

It is really harder to believe in murder
Than to believe in cancer. Cancer is here:
The lump, the dull pain, the occasional sickness:
Murder a reversal of sleep and waking.
Murder was there. Your ordinary murderer
Regards himself as an innocent victim.
To himself he is still what he used to be
Or what he would be. He cannot realize
That everything is irrevocable,
The past unredeemable. But cancer, now,
That is something real.

—T. S. Eliot, *The Family Reunion*

I have spoken of our "generic guilt," as something that comes into being with our freedom—a heard accusation on the part of the psychic womb as it parts to let us out. I have said that this has to be distinguished from sin, in that it is characterized by independence rather than by transgression. But now we have to see how this generic guilt, while distinct from sin, relates to it.

---

3. Max Scheler, *Ressentiment* (Milwaukee, WI: Marquette University Press, 1994).

First, let us define *sin*. This is an exercise of our independence in a way that injures another person or society. Now the relationship between generic guilt and sin consists in this: that the already present sense of being guiltily on my own makes the sinful act something that "comes naturally" to me. I am already this private being, so why not go all the way with this "me-for-me" condition? The act of sin does not appear *to me* in its stark destructiveness. I do not see it primarily in the context of the order with which it breaks. I feel it as a natural emanation of my privacy. Its context is my atmosphere as a private being, in which it fits, not the order that it disrupts. Or—what comes to the same thing—the order itself is seen rather as that primitive enclosing order, the psychic womb, with which I *have* to break in order to realize my freedom at all.

Van Breemen, in *As Bread That Is Broken*, has a brilliant analysis of the sin of David over Bathsheba. The affair starts with David, the extroverted warrior, who is hot and can't sleep. There's nothing wrong with that, says Van Breemen. Of course, there isn't. It is ordinary consciousness, and it is the sense of me-for-me. It is the guilty privacy of an ordinary man. But it will be the justifying base for all that follows. For next comes the sight of the girl bathing. (Well, I'm a man aren't I, and a king to boot!) And so, one thing leads to another. The adultery is beautiful. In David's consciousness, it represents the original "me-for-me" now broadened out into a river of delight. Thus, the original justifying context is enlarged—so enlarged, so beautiful, so engulfing, that it makes natural the summoning of Uriah back from the front to give David a firsthand account of how the campaign is going. Then the attempt to get Uriah to sleep with his wife, and, when this fails, the expanded plot of David's inner drama makes natural the plan to eliminate Uriah, involving Joab and an unwarranted tactical risk. Joab foresees that the soldier in David will be angry at this needless risk until he hears that Uriah has been killed, and so it turns out.

So enmeshed is David's whole act, for David, in the original self-justifying context, that the prophet Nathan has to use an indirect method to fish it out from this subjective sea and present it in all its enormity as getting a man killed to get his wife. He tells the story of the rich man plundering the poor man of his one lamb. In that figure, David is presented with an act of sin *without* its subjective justifying context, and he positively shakes with moral indignation. Then he is caught, for Nathan has only to say, "That man is you."

What I want to emphasize here is David's justifying context, and what I want to suggest is that this justifying context justifies *because* it is itself a guilty state in the generic sense of *guilty*. Somewhere inside is the little voice that says, "Well, you're on your own, you know." It is this sense of being somehow originally outlawed that, albeit very inexplicit, grounds our evil deeds, and, when they come, gives them growing and beauty in our eyes. The self that I *consult*, when I proceed to what is possibly a very wicked deed, is *already* "offside and content to be so." Thus, the generic guilt that, contrasted with adultery and murder, must be judged innocent, *drawn into consultation* becomes a principal actor in the drama.

Moralists have always been intrigued and puzzled by the small beginnings of big sins. But they easily miss the point, here, and describe the small beginnings as a "proneness to evil," and warn us to watch out for "our sinful nature" in its very earliest stirrings. There is, of course, a practical common sense at work here. Still, the point is missed. For the point is only grasped by attending to the puzzling character of the process. The point is that we *find ourselves* doing harm, rather than initiating the harmful act in an obvious way. St. Paul says precisely this, in one passage that everyone remembers because it is so astonishingly rare of its kind in moral literature. And we puzzle ourselves in doing harm because of that peculiar base in consciousness from which we operate, precisely because, I mean, there's no harm *in the base itself* yet it has limitless power to justify evil actions, or at least to keep them soft in our eyes. It's really got us foxed, this bipolar structure of "innocent guilt" and sinful act.

Nor is this to mitigate or to soften the evil in sin. Quite the contrary, it is to bring our attention to the real nature of sin, which lies not in "rebellion against God" but in the peculiar dialogue of alienated man with himself. Sin is the sealing of alienation, its total normalizing. Hannah Arendt's phrase "the banality of evil," fearlessly used in connection with the concentration camps, which less morally perceptive people can only describe with superlatives of malevolence, is entirely apposite here. The godlessness of man is not rebellion against God but, just what the word says, God-less-ness. It is that peculiar me-for-me condition in which alone freedom can get going. It is the human beginning-without-God, the consideration of which generates the paradox of a God who apparently creates man to fall and be redeemed.

The error of the "moralists" referred to consists in understanding the base (generic guilt) in terms of the evil deed, instead of the other way around. They stretch the evil deed back, back, back, to a sort of mini-evil-deed, a homunculus of evil, instead of grappling—as a few do—with the puzzling nature of the base, that tantalizing quasi-equation of guilt with loneliness. Of course, the "other way around" is much more difficult to handle, but only so can we open the ethical picture to its theological dimension.

But there is a vital further step to this argument. That very guilt, which lets sin come easily and legitimates it in our consciousness, is what generates the feeling that there can be no radical forgiveness. The very on-my-own-ness that I consult to ease my way into sin will be my unavowed reason for hoping for no forgiveness. I may *say*, "How can I be forgiven for this murder?" but what I am really saying is, "How can *I*, who did a thing like that, be forgiven?" What I am really looking at is not simply the murder, but the murder *colored* by my guilty self-awareness. A person's sins become for him an enlarged version of an original loneliness. Originally, the sin hid in the generic guilt. Now the generic guilt hides in the sin and makes of the latter a typical manifestation of my lonely, estranged self. Thus, the original justifier of sin becomes its accuser.

But its accuser in a half-hearted way. For as long as I feel unforgivable I am still clinging to my sin *as* a typical manifestation of myself. I am still *coloring* it with my lonely selfhood. And *that* means that I am not fully *acknowledging* my sin. Strange as it may seem, there is a difference between saying, "Good God, *I* did *that*" and saying, "Of course I did that, what else can you expect?" What is strange is that it is the former that is the real confession of sin and not the latter, despite the latter's apparently greater humility. The latter way of speaking is not a confession of sin but a posturing of "the sinner," and the real intention of this posturing is to maintain, as a kind of last-ditch defense, some of the *justifying* force of the generic guilt. People do this. They confess their sins orgiastically to maintain themselves in their proud and frightened solitude, and the capital point here is that the self is being kept in a state of osmosis with the original self-sense that is pervaded with the generic guilt. And this because the thing above all feared is the exposure of the self to the love that is the self's true climate.

That's what the gospel is about. What Jesus seeks in each of us is the frightened shivering creature which, before any of us can remember, huddled into the garment of guilt which the psychic womb wove for it as its only protection against the rude wind of an unknown love. The psychic womb is the God who sewed those leaves together to hide our first identity. The gospel is going back to that beginning of us and calling us out into our end.

In short, the source of sin in us is not a homunculus of

evil in us; it is a lonely frightened being whom the cosmos has chased into the isolation that we know as man.

Thus, our analysis brings us to the most radical understanding of the self, to the confession of what Eliot calls "the essential sickness or strength of the human soul."[4] I am, in my deepest identity, self-transcending. I deny myself, and therefore God, in saying that I am on my own. This denial is the human guilt that only an incomprehensible love can dissolve. It is done incomprehensibly on a gibbet. Imprisoned by guilt, I am liberated by love. Guilt *is* imprisonment. I am that extraordinary creature, of whom love, coming to me and awoken in me, is the purging. And only a relentlessly prosecuted understanding of the self as self-transcending can do justice to the existential identity of "coming to me" and "awoken in me" and to the labor of this redeeming.

EPILOGUE

My epilogue is the description of a prayer in which this whole drama of the self is enacted. It is taken from *The Last Western* by Thomas S. Klise, being the description of "The Listening Prayer" as practiced by the Silent Servants of the Used, Abused, and Utterly Screwed-up.

> It is of the essence of the listening prayer that the listener put himself away from the pleas and suggestions of the normal self, especially when a life-giving action seems the recommended course, for the normal self will suggest many false deeds for the sake of pride or guilt removal or vengeance or for the satisfaction of desires that go back to the time before love spoke.

---

4. T. S. Eliot writing of Blake in *The Sacred Wood: Essays on Poetry and Criticism* (London: Methuen & Co., 1920), 88.

In all true listening the listener opens his spirit to the Loving One, the Power and the Strength as some call Him-Her, the YOU, who is wholly Other and yet also wedded to the true self. And it is of the essence and perfection of true listening that once the demands of the normal self have been completely put aside, the voice of the self wedded to Truth and Love speak in such a way to the heart of the listener that he is assured it is not other than the voice of the Loving One Him-Herself. And the listener knows this with the exact same degree of certainty that he knows that he exists.

Gloss of Marion Byrne: Has nothing to do with the lying and insanity of hearing voices, as the Fools of Spain believed. Entirely a matter of opening self completely to Other so that Other might enter and be joined to self so that when self speaks, it is the Other speaking in true wedlock, with utter clarity even though the language may be obscure to the normal self and even unknown to the mental workings of the normal self.

In any situation where the sacrifice of one's own life is required, one realizes it with a serene joy and absolute confidence because the road is so clearly marked, and there is never any doubt. If there is hesitation or confusion, the purest listening is required.

EXPLANATORY NOTE

Some definition of "the lover" is called for. I would suggest that the lover is one whose well-being consists, and is experienced as consisting, in willing the well-being of another. Now there are many experiences to which normal usage would accord the name of love that do not answer to that definition. The heavily romantic form of love for instance. Nevertheless, these experiences, though they don't fit my definition, are judged by it and found wanting. The romantic lover has not yet discovered what love is all about, and this means he has not yet discovered how *he* loves. "How I love" and "who I am" are one identical discovery. He has not yet discovered *himself* in the act of loving. For him, the act of loving is an act of self-forgetfulness, of inattention, of chosen dreaming. In other words, the condition of willing another's flourishing is precisely a condition in which I am newly in touch with myself. "Newly" is vague. The change is crucial. The new self-awareness is revelatory.

Thus, the Goldsmith[5] progression through the five stages of affectivity ending with the agapic is precisely the process of coming to myself, of the emergence of the real self into conscious volition and control. It is the progress of myself as lover through the necessary confusions and dead ends to clarity. In the same way, progress in prayer, according to Abbot Chapman, passes through desiring to will what God wills to willing what God wills. The desire is already controlled, confusedly (and how confusedly! almost imperceptibly) by the emergent will whose "successful" operation, it is already very dimly perceived, is to move in harmony with the transcendent and all-controlling will.

There is a section heading in Austin Farrer's difficult book *Finite and Infinite* called "Will the clue to the nature of desire." This has always fascinated me. I felt that I knew and did not know what it meant. That meaning is now clear. Desire cannot make ultimate sense as "desire for something." It is desire for a subjective condition, and the subjective condition is "willing," and willing—unlike desire which is for that which is not—is of

---

5. Taken from unpublished notes by Charles Goldsmith, PhD.

that which is, independently of myself. To that happy condition, desire tends. From that happy condition, desire gets its nature and meaning.

Ignatius describes a condition of "consolation without a cause." It is for him an experience of grace. He says it can only come from God. My analysis of this condition would be that in it I experience myself as happy precisely as willing. I experience will as the term or end of desire. In the customary order, desire explains willing, motivates the will, and happiness consists in having got, by willing, what I desired. In the deeper order that is here operative, happy willing seeks, and can receive, no explanation outside itself, no explanation in terms of something desired. Nor is this a question of some inner well-being or well-functioning operating in isolation. On the contrary, it is precisely the oneness of willing with attunement to an independent reality that is the substance of the delight. In this delight, will is *identified* as willing that which independently is, *I* am identified as willing that which is. In this experience I know myself as self-transcendent, and this is not a knowing something *about myself*; it is the knowing *of myself*.

In the experience of maturely loving another person, I am in touch with myself, but I cannot then say that apart from this experience I have no self, no being. There is still, for me, a substantial self, a principle of continuity that would continue to support me were this love to be no more. Whereas in the experience described by Ignatius, I know that "outside this, I am nothing. Outside this, I am not." In those privileged moments when the essence of willing is laid bare, I know that all-controlling, independent will, outside of which I have no being.

Considering this clarification of my meaning of the lover, I would say that the reason why the experience of radical forgiveness is crucial to our salvation is that, in this experience, the step into the self's being as lover is taken in the only way that embraces the whole reality of our existential condition. All other steps into selfhood are shortcuts. It is the self as immemorially pervaded by generic guilt that has to rise with Christ from the dead of sin.